Human Resource
Strategies in China

Human Resource Strategies in China

Alma Whiteley
Curtin University of Technology, Australia

Sara Cheung
*Hong Kong Institute of
Human Resource Management, Hong Kong*

Zhang Shi Quan
International Technology and Economy Institute, China

World Scientific
Singapore • New Jersey • London • Hong Kong

3-14-02

Published by

World Scientific Pub

P O Box 128, Farrer ~~Road, Singapore 912805~~

USA office: Suite 1B, 1060 Main Street, River Edge, NJ 07661

UK office: 57 Shelton Street, Covent Garden, London WC2H 9HE

British Library Cataloguing-in-Publication Data
A catalogue record for this book is available from the British Library.

HUMAN RESOURCE STRATEGIES IN CHINA

ISBN 981-02-3840-1

Printed in Singapore.

CONTENTS

1. INTRODUCTION   **1**
Characteristics of the open door policy   3
One policy: Two systems, PRC and FIEs   5
Human resource management strategies and practices in
    foreign invested enterprises in the PRC: The 1996 study   12
The development of a new pattern of thinking   16

2. IDEOLOGY IN CONTEXT   **25**
Western ideology: The business inheritance   25
Chinese ideology   32
The economic context   39
Impacts of the open door policy in China   42

**3. HUMAN RESOURCES IN THE CONTEXT OF
BUSINESS STRATEGY**   **55**
Human resources in the context of business strategy   55
Human resource management in the West   60
Human resource management strategies and practices in
    foreign invested enterprises in the PRC: The 1997 study   67
Business strategy theory and concepts   68
Business strategy findings   76

**4. HUMAN RESOURCE STRATEGIES IN THE
CHINESE CONTEXT**   **89**
Human resource strategies in the Chinese context   89
Fundamental personnel management model   99
Transition to the human resource management model   101
Sophisticated human resource management model   104
Human resource strategy findings   106

**5. THE ROLE OF THE HR FUNCTION IN FOREIGN
INVESTED ENTERPRISES**   **115**
The role of the HR function in foreign invested enterprises   115
Human resource practices   118

6. **THE GREATEST DIRECTNESS IS FLEXIBLE-COMPATIBLE PARADIGMS**   **169**

Compatible paradigms: Complex adaptive systems and Chinese
    relational systems   169
Complex adaptive systems   174
Characteristics of CAS   175
Chinese relational system   179
The need for a catalyst   182

7. **REFERENCES**   **185**

INDEX   **195**

1.   Introduction

We have come together, three authors, one from the West and two from Hong Kong and Beijing to bring to you our ideas and research into human resource strategy in China. We share a passion. We are committed to the rise of a new regimen for managing people within the Chinese setting. We recognize that the linear, rational, analytic, systems-oriented Western business methods have much to offer good strategic human resource management. However we also see that the more holistic, relational, interactive adaptive systems of Chinese tradition have an important role to play, especially as we enter a more fluid business future. In the case of those who want to do business in China it is the Chinese tradition that must be the superordinate influence, for the primary reason that business is being conducted within the Chinese cultural and economic setting.

The focus of this book is on human resource strategies in China, particularly in relation to Foreign Invested Enterprises (FIEs). Contributions from human resource managers, chief executives and other managers operating in China have provided us with knowledge and insight into actual practices of FIEs in the People's Republic of China (PRC). Like the study reported in Rosen (1999), a methodology was chosen for studies in 1996 and 1997 that helped us learn about human resource management in China (Tang, 1996; Whiteley, Cheung, Zhang & So, 1997).

FIEs are of particular interest when one looks at world trade. A family of worldwide trading partners has come into being. Variously known as conglomerates, multi nationals, or global organizations, these organizations, often grossing more than the GDP of small countries, have to somehow balance the need for a central hub with that of local requirements. As far back as 1993 there were already 11 000 multinational corporations with more than 100 000 affiliated companies operating in world trade (Cheng &

1

Lu, 1993). Of special interest to the authors and research teams in our study of FIE human resource management strategies and practices in the PRC is the design of human resource and development systems to facilitate what Wu (1992:9) calls the "soft national capacity" associated with such a large number of enterprises.

The macro-economic scene described by Tang (1996) suggests that the PRC has gradually become a significant economy with which to trade. According to the latest figures, China accounts for approximately 3% of world trade and it is expected that entry into the World Trade Organization will further 'kickstart' the Chinese economy (Callick, 1999). Furthermore, growth of the economy has in recent years been spectacular, showing an annual increase of at least 12% of total national product in the period 1995-1997, a higher rate than both developed and developing countries (see figure 1).

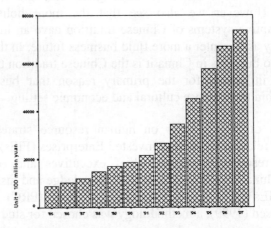

Figure 1. Total National Product of The People's Republic of China

Source: China Statistical Yearbook (1998)

Annual trade has increased from over US$60 billion in 1985 to US$325.1 billion in 1997 with much of the growth due to the national policy of opening the PRC up to international trade and investment. The extent to which the PRC is committed to the open door policy is evident by its dependence on foreign trade for 36% of the national economy in 1997. The

PRC's market driven economy is influenced by four factors - *economic growth* (the industrial output value of Sino-foreign joint ventures, cooperative businesses and exclusively foreign-owned enterprises was 8.6% of the nation's total industrial output value); *free pricing strategy* (to allow market forces to dictate supply and demand pricing); *market development* (with a free market system); and a *legal system* that regulates, controls and administers the economy.

President Jiang has officially pointed out that China would never sacrifice its national interests in order to gain membership to the WTO (Callick, 1999), Equally however, the PRC has shown its willingness to integrate with foreign economies by allowing foreign investment to about 11% total fixed assets investment. From the point of view of investors this allowance makes a statement about the PRC's perceived viability as a major economy in terms of providing reliable, long term markets. Additionally, as the most populous nation on Earth with a population of around 1.24 billion a third crucial factor for investment is the large potential of consumer markets.

As confidence increases in the ability of FIEs to take advantage of the open door policy to serve growing parts of China, it becomes important to consider key current and longer-term infrastructure arrangements. In the human resource context, this includes developing strategies for human resource (manpower) planning, recruitment and retention, compensation, training and management education. We describe these strategies in later chapters. These developments need to be viewed first against the backdrop of some of the characteristics of the open door policy and secondly against some central issues for China concerning the open door policy.

Characteristics of the open door policy

Tang, Cheng, Lai, and Zhang (1996) describe some of the recent measures taken as part of the open door policy system. A vital point to note is that the motives of government and FIEs are inevitably different. The Chinese government's policy on the allocation of manpower pays more attention to economic and social stability, fair employment and to minimizing unemployment. Even though the tolerance for unemployment is higher than in the past, a government that is facing somewhere near 20-plus million unemployed from the state sector by 2000 (Rosen, 1999) wants to persuade FIEs to absorb surplus labor. In a country where the headcount has traditionally been a measure of power and importance, Chinese partners might often share the government's approach. This somewhat contradicts the strategy of FIEs who appear to be putting an emphasis mainly on economic profit, efficiency and productivity in their joint or, more recently, wholly owned foreign enterprises.

It is very evident both from the 1997 interviews conducted by the authors as well as other data, that FIEs are not too concerned with involving themselves in what Rosen (1999:91) calls China's astounding social dilemma.

> *"Foreign investors...insist on screening out unskilled workers or "lifers", and create retraining or placement centers to redirect unneeded staff. As the market for such services grows, capable human resource consultants have emerged to help FIEs deal with overstaffing. Whether these adjustment mechanisms will successfully reallocate excess workers to new jobs or just shuffle them out of the FIE's in-box to an unspecified future is not clear (Rosen, 1999:93).*

The PRC government continues to open its "door" more widely and expansively, and in doing so, some might say, leaves itself increasingly vulnerable to labor market instability. It has recently established an "active, rational and effective" (superseding the "active but careful") strategy. Here, *active* means actively seeking more foreign funds to replenish insufficient resources and improve resource quality. *Rational* refers to rationally guiding foreign investment. *Effective* relates to the optimization of the benefits of using foreign funds. To this end the government has issued various policies, codes and guidelines. These include the 1994-1995 Policy Program on State Industries in the 1990s, the Provisions for Guiding the Direction of Foreign Investment, the Guiding Catalogue for Foreign Investment and other related guidelines. In keeping with its needs, the PRC has encouraged foreign investment in agricultural technology, energy and communication, and other technological high content and labor intensive industries. Air transport, foreign trade, insurance, audit and legal consultation sectors, newly opened up, will extend the PRC's tertiary and quatenary profile.

The need of FIEs for a stable and comprehensive legal and regulatory system is recognized by the PRC. In line with this, as well as with the PRC's own government policy, laws are being promulgated and circulated swiftly. In the findings of one study however (Cheng & Zhang, 1995) a strong theme emerged suggesting that although laws were being passed, there was a lag in their interpretation and adoption by employers and workers. Conversely, we received reports that FIEs were quite prepared to reinterpret these laws for personal gain. This does not only mean financial gain but psychological and cultural gain as well as is seen by comments such as that of Rosen (1999): "[Western] management in general," says Rosen, "must fight against ancient culture and tradition, which diverge fundamentally from Western workplace habits".

Laws on unfair competition and labor law are recent and the latter is comprehensive and progressive by previous standards. A current task of the Chinese government is to complete and extend some of these laws to all the provinces and cities. The concern for a 'national treatment' policy towards FIEs is currently being addressed. To fulfil the needs of the PRC, FIEs will need to play an active role in helping achieve a stable macro economy. An aim of the ninth Five-year plan was to maintain inflation at 10% - FIE salary arrangements will need to take this into account (see chapter 5 for some of the difficulties in keeping salaries down when needing to recruit talent). As the FIE and PRC story unfolds, the challenge presented becomes one of managing these tensions and contradictions.

One Policy: Two Systems, PRC and FIEs

Within China every business is subject to overall economic development policy. However when considering FIEs it is clear that there are two separate systems in operation, each with their distinctive characteristics. These characteristics are suggested in table 1 below (taken from Sweeney, 1996).

DIMENSION	CHINESE PARTNER	FOREIGN PARTNER
Financial Outcomes	Increase foreign exchange reserves	Long-term repatriation of profits
	Invest for the future developments	Minimise potential loss
		Long-term profit maximization in shortest possible time
Investment	Minimum initial investment	Acceptable minimum investment
Negotiation	Holistic	Sequential
	Heuristic	Incremental
	Flexible	Binding
Contract	Adaptable	Enforceable
	Short-term	Long-term precise
	Ambiguous	Unambiguous
Planning	Congruence between state plan and IBV	Maximum flexibility
Inputs	Focus on domestic suppliers	Minimize poor quality
		Minimize unpredictability
Outputs	Generate foreign exchange	Access Chinese domestic market
	Increase exports	
	Increase technical knowledge	Develop Chinese domestic market
	Independence	
Strategy	Short-term/medium-term	Short-term/long-term
	Domestic/international	Domestic/international
Operations	Stress on quality	Stress on quality
Personnel	Maximum number of local employees	Fewest people possible for acceptable output
	Long term training of personnel	Maximum productivity

	Long-term increase in payment to personnel	Low turnover
Management	Traditional	Modern
	Inflexible within the IBV context	Flexible

Table 1. Characteristics of Foreign Invested Enterprises

Source: Sweeney, E. Human resource management implications of managing business change in China. *Proceedings of the Second South China International Business Symposium, Macau* page 897, 1996.

The nature of Sweeney's study results in a polarization of attitudes between Chinese and international businesses. This is understandable when trying to describe and understand contrasting approaches. Care needs to be taken however, in how such data is used. In practice, for example, changes in the labor law have been introduced for wider purposes by the Chinese government. This suggests that the legal infrastructure within which human resource management operates will, in some respects, soon resemble that of Western countries.

When studying the history of personnel management in China it is clear that such a similarity has not always been the case. Zhao's (1996) description is very useful in shaping a backdrop to the current human resource issues facing both FIEs and national development policy makers tasked with achieving the dual aims of social/economic and human resource development (see table 2).

Year	Stage of Personnel Management	Characteristics
1949-1959	Preliminary Stage	Fixed employment; state monopoly for recruitment and labor allocation
1952-1957	Beginning Stage	Soviet management model with

		authoritarian leadership; piece rate wages; merit-oriented payment
1957-1966	Development Stage	Chief leader responsibility system; committees with employee delegation; democratic management with employee participation
1966-1976 (Cultural Revolution)	Stagnation Stage	"3 irons" policy strengthened
1978-	Reform Stage	Personnel management system is reformed; theories and practices of human resource management are initiated

Table 2. The History of Personnel Management Systems in Chinese Enterprises

Source: Zhao, S. Human resource management implications of managing business change in China. *Proceedings of the Second South China International Business Symposium, Macau* page 963, 1996

In 1949, Zhao tells us, faced with finding jobs for more than a million people, the (then) government began to help by not only finding jobs for people, but by encouraging others to find their own jobs, and allocating jobs to those as necessary. The next thirty years or so saw an increase in the awareness of the need for specialist functions and expertise in the people management area, in the early years using the Soviet central administration approach. This was realized through the Communist Party structure involving Party regulation and delegation of powers to enterprise-based committees. Zhao mentions some of these regulations including the policy of "liang can yi gai san jie he". This policy meant that "workers should participate in administration; cadres participate in production; reform untenable regulations; integrate leaders with technical personnel and workers to solve technical problems" (Zhao 1996:964). A 'lessons learned' approach was taken across China, aimed at producing a national memory of experiences and lessons from enterprises.

From 1966 and for the next ten years or more, a strategy was selected which was to alter the flow of personnel management development in enterprises. Ideological and social as well as entrepreneurial considerations were taken into account when reforming enterprise arrangements. The planned central economy, administered by the State, employed a system of government agency. This included traditional personnel functions such as allocation of employees, a central differentiation of roles and jobs, and a protectionist approach in State and collective enterprises.

Protectionism, and with it expectations of security in almost every aspect of work and home life developed into what Khong and Trigo (1996:953) called the 'iron rice bowl' attitude. They described this as "a phrase used to express a safe job-for-life through non-differentiated rewards in a state-owned firm". Zhao (1996:965) talked about the "three irons" - the iron rice bowl, the iron chair and the iron pay. The iron metaphor meant ironcast. The bowl metaphor meant a foodpot where sustenance would be guaranteed. Iron pay meant that pay did not rest on successful performance and competition but could be counted on in good times and bad. Iron chair meant the reliance on a position not being taken away. As Zhao pointed out, problems included "severe boundaries that are created between cadres and workers...cadres can be promoted but never be demoted, leading to a surplus of unproductive personnel...the administrative method which relies heavily on diplomacy and relationships in selecting and recruiting personnel, hardly follows the principle of 'selecting the good and sifting out the bad" (Zhao, 1996:965). Iron pay, he suggested, also called 'da guo fan' or 'everyone eats from the same pot' meant that there was more interest in even distribution of wages than in rewarding merit or stimulating initiative.

The three irons were consistent with the strategic and national goals of the PRC as it developed through this phase. These strategies included broadening the base of employable people, producing stability and confidence, redistributing cultural hegemony from intellectual to practical and gradually to a mix of the two (following the cultural revolution). However, once the decision was made to change the framework of relationships between enterprises and government (Cheng, et al., 1995) and to embrace an advanced market economy through an open door policy, sweeping human resource reforms were needed.

These were, and still are, forthcoming. In particular, from the 1980's, the human resource concept began to replace that of personnel administration where placement, control and protection predominated (see chapter 3). Areas such as the contract method of employment, job placements (where the State included the labor department, groups, and people in the planning and administration of placements) were reformed. Cooperatives and privately owned enterprises were approved, together with recognition of the need for improved productivity through the overhaul of human resource systems such as compensation and remuneration, recruitment and selection, management development and training (see chapter 5).

Since the 1990's, state determination to extend the change from a planned economy to a mixed economy in key areas such as human resource management has become evident internally through devices such as the 1995 Labor Law (Markel, 1994).

Employment protection legislation has been rapidly growing, the idea being to eventually match that of developed countries. Legislation has included legally binding employment contracts, working hours (five day, forty hour week), safety and welfare at work, female and child protection, social insurance, workers rights to apply for jobs and a nationally governed minimum wage. These have represented radical infrastructure changes. Mutual employment protection meant that whilst employees had rights, such as the right to be trained, heard in disputes, provided for in insurance and so on, they also faced accountabilities. They had to fulfil the labor bargain by doing tasks, improving their skills, and obeying safety, health and discipline laws. It was this accountability that was, in the short term, likely to prove culturally resistant.

The side products of the state-controlled system seemed to be that order and stability were gained at a cost of optimal human initiative, motivation, and effort. In particular, drawing on the Tang, et al. (1996) study and other human resource management studies of the 1990s, there was a major latent effect of the protected situation of the 1960s - 1970s. This was and still is carried forward in some areas to the 1990s. This was most easily seen in the erosion of the need to consider quality and innovation as driving forces in the labor bargain. Due to the negative view of things intellectual, energies and strategies for aggressively developing technology were not part of the Chinese economic strategy in the 1970s and 1980s. (Cheng & Lu, 1993, Cheng, et al., 1995). This also needs to be borne in mind when making judgements about human resourcing needs and issues in the PRC.

One of the consequences of a developing workforce has been the perceived availability of cheap (and somewhat pliable) labor. This has been an attraction for FIEs notwithstanding the problems of productivity and skill levels that come with such a situation. Quality of manpower is directly related to a nation's level of education. Although China is attending to this, still, around 11.6% of the population are illiterate or semi-illiterate, with 34.8% at primary school level, and only 3.5% with a college degree or higher (China Statistical Yearbook, 1998). This, as well as an industry structure dominated by primary (50%) and secondary (24%) labor distribution, has been reflected in performance at work – the result is poor performance and products that do not meet required standards.

Because of the open door policy and with it the exposure to foreign invested enterprises, an external as well as internal force has been making a significant impact on the human resource situation in the PRC. Some of this can be seen to be immediately beneficial as business and human resource management skills come into the PRC from organizations that have already done much of their learning, are successful and are ready to share. Some can be seen as challenging, such as the relative disadvantage faced by the State-owned enterprise (SOE) in competing in the marketplace for high quality technicians and administrative personnel. Hong Kong has long suffered this (Tang & Whiteley, 1990) and the consequences of wages and talent drift has soon become a serious problem, especially when organizations invest heavily in training those who then 'job-hop'. The beginning of this phenomenon has already been reported as happening in the PRC and it is discussed further in the section on recruitment and selection in chapter 5.

Cheng, et al. (1995) calls this situation "vying" and Tang (1996) points out that whilst there are 200 million unemployed in the PRC, FIEs only employ about 11% of the number employed in State-owned enterprises.

Even then, FIEs are only interested in the trained or trainable. Thus FIEs are not really helping to resolve the unemployment problem. An interpretation of Wu (1992)'s reasons for changing jobs, suggests that with 31% of job changes being income-related and 11% being welfare-related, there is some degree of job-hopping. Such figures are supported by Khong et al. (1996:956) who found that employees in Guangzhou saw high salary and reward, and good welfare treatment, as the two highest demands from work. Whoever can supply such extrinsic factors may best be able to succeed in recruiting.

In a study of some units in the Guangdong province, 45% of workers wished to be transferred to non-state-owned units (Khong, et al., 1996). Whilst this remains problematic for the PRC development plan, there are still some other problems to be overcome. These include one-way mobility to cities with a resulting strain on infrastructure and resources, residence regulation impediments, and the problem of training and development responsibility in a high turnover labor market. Some of these issues should nevertheless be good news for FIEs as it appears over the last five years that the PRC is adapting, modifying and regulating in order for the way to be smoothed for incoming enterprises.

Human Resource Management Strategies and Practices in Foreign Invested Enterprises in the PRC: The 1996 study

The discussion above explains why there was an urgent need to continue to study the business and human resource strategies of FIEs operating in the PRC. To obtain a feeling for what these strategies were, how they were aligned with each other, and most importantly, how they were introduced to the PRC economy, the authors conducted two studies. The first, "Human Resource Management Strategies and Practices in Foreign Invested Enterprises in the People's Republic of China" was a quantitative study carried out in late 1995, sponsored by the Hong Kong Institute of Human Resource Management (HKIHRM) and the International Technology & Economy Institute of Development Research Center of the State Council (ITEI). The second study was sponsored by the above organizations together with Curtin University in Australia. This was a qualitative follow-up, providing in depth responses to selected areas of interest.

Of particular interest were the strategic responses of FIEs and their perceived priorities and problems in the human resource field. In order to comment on the 'fit' of FIEs with Chinese requirements, the quantitative study sought to ascertain how FIEs transported their concepts of strategic human resource arrangements into their operations in China.

A questionnaire was designed to investigate the background information of the respondents; their strategic orientation; organizational performance, human resource management approaches and human resource management practices. These areas were targeted to ensure adequate investigation of the integration of business strategy with human resource strategy and the subsequent impact on organizational performance.

The sampling frame consisted of 150 Institute of Human Resource Management (IHRM) members who had establishments in the PRC, 560 firms identified by ITEI, 145 firms who were members of various Chambers of Commerce in Hong Kong, 740 firms from the mailing list of China International Business Investigation Co. Ltd., 177 firms from the China Large Foreign Invested Enterprises Catalogue and 14 firms who were participants in the pre-survey conference.

The profile of responding organizations was skewed in favor of large and medium manufacturing organizations predominantly owned by United States, Hong Kong, PRC and European organizations who operated mainly in Beijing, Shanghai and Guangdong. Around 11% of the 1 450 organizations targeted responded to the questionnaire.

Data analysis was divided into two parts. The first part aimed to uncover the business and human resource management strategies used by FIEs in the PRC. With respect to business strategy typologies, Porter's model (Porter, 1980) was used for categorisation. Companies were classified as pursuing any one of the following typologies: Quality Strategy, Cost Reduction Strategy, Innovation Strategy, Quality and Cost Reduction Strategy.

Part two of the analysis focused on the identification of the patterns of HRM practices in the PRC. Frequency distribution tables were constructed for each of the practices. In addition, data was analysed to identify correlations between HRM practices and size, industry and nationality of ownership. For this analysis, companies were categorised in terms of size of company, type of industry, and nationality of ownership.

The notion that human resource management played a central role in FIEs in the PRC was borne out by the results of the quantitative survey. Over 90% had a human resource management function (see table 3) and around 90% had a director or senior person responsible for human resources (see table 4).

	Percentage		
	Large	**Small**	**All**
Yes	94.9	83.7	91.2
No	5.1	16.3	8.8

Table 3. Presence of a Specialist Human Resource Function at Establishment

	Percentage		
	Large	**Small**	**All**
Yes	92.0	85.7	89.9
No	8.0	14.3	10.1

Table 4. Presence of a Director or Someone at the Highest Level of the Organisation with Specific Responsibility for the HR Function

Based on the idea that FIEs would usually adopt a particular strategy for business competitiveness, Porter's (1980) suggestion that these might include innovation, cost reduction or quality enhancement was adopted as a theme to investigate business strategies in the PRC, and was followed through in the qualitative study.

Three major strategic choices were factored out of the responses from the FIEs. These were *a Strategic HRM approach; a Development-focus HRM approach* and *an Internal-focus HRM approach.*

The *Strategic HR approach* was described as one in which
- HR functions and activities were highly devolved to line managers and departments
- HR functions were heavily involved in major strategic decisions made
- HRM was determined by formal and explicit planning procedures and it was closely linked to business planning
- Performance appraisal systems were highly integrated with other HR systems and there was a broad career path with comparatively high basic pay and salary levels.

The *Development-focus HR* approach was one in which
- Training was a valued function
- There was a long term view and this applied to training and development objectives with line managers highly involved
- There was great effort made to persuade new employees to commit to the organization's values and expected behaviors
- Performance appraisal was integrated with other systems and there were long-term assessment criteria used and multiple career ladders offered.

The *Internal-focus HR* approach (Factor 3) was one in which
- There was high job security
- Line managers were heavily involved in the planning of T & D activities
- Job descriptions were explicitly defined and job vacancies were filled from internal sources

A further analysis revealed that organizations tended to use multiple approaches to implement their human resource services.

There were three typologies of business strategy in operation. Around 36.5% used quality enhancement and cost reduction as their business strategy. Around 22% used quality enhancement and innovation and 39 % used all three as the competitive business strategy. Quality enhancement seemed to be the 'strategy in common' but there was widespread use of multiple strategies. The quality enhancement strategic choice was understandable, given the current situation concerning qualified and quality-conscious personnel in the PRC. Adopting multiple strategies was at odds with the conventional wisdom of one dominant competitive strategy usually giving a competitive advantage (Porter, 1980). Perhaps FIEs did not have a strong focus for the Chinese situation. Alternatively, it was possible that the developing and changing nature of the legal and regulatory system meant a more interchangeable strategy was needed, or that there was an interdependence in the three strategies that was found to be more forceful than Porter and others' suggestion of a single focus. This finding was borne out after analysis of data on FIEs' belief that business strategy together with HR strategy would make a difference in organizational performance (such as market share, return on sales and sales growth). Again, combinations of strategy and HR types were connected to differences in performance.

The picture that was beginning to emerge in the quantitative study was that of FIEs who were using quality as a strategic anchor, thereby entering into a natural strategic liaison with the human resource function. Within human resource areas, FIEs were showing a responsiveness to the uncertainties of labor supply (and perhaps labor regulation) by mixing internal and externally focused strategies and taking a long term, developmental approach to the training and development of staff to fulfil the quality enhancement strategy.

The development of a new pattern of thinking

In a qualitative follow-up of the 1996 study, (Whiteley et al., 1997 - see chapter 3) we noted that there was a sense of the foreign partner superimposing methodologies on the existing business framework. We suggested that instead it would be better to co create a new business modus operandi, one that allowed the rational and relational to co exist. The image that came to our minds was conceptualized as a "1+1 = 3" evolutionary model. For this to come about, "a period of learning is needed so that shared understanding and mutual respect for each other can transcend business transactions" (Whiteley, et al., 1997:88).

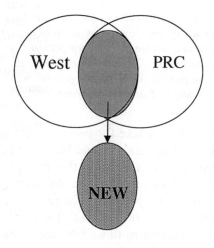

Figure 2. Co creating traditions

In the co-creation model, (figure 2) the Western tradition could contribute something (but not all) of its linear and rational self to intersect with the Chinese tradition. The Chinese would bring its holistic and relational self. The intersection would constitute the 'new reality'. The intent would be not to superimpose one tradition over the other but to co-create a new way of doing things, producing a new set of traditions. Before too long there would be an optimal synergy. In the foreign case, the power of business experience and acumen would benefit from the Chinese power of a large consumer market. It is proposed in chapter 6 that the rational economic model of management, together with the Protestant work ethic, is unlikely to continue to work in the Western world. New technologies, electronic communication and the impacts these will have on almost every facet of business means that institutionalized, standardized, formalized and stabilized structures, systems and processes will no longer serve business competitiveness. In chapter 6 an emerging paradigm based on the notion of complex adaptive systems in business will be presented as being harmonious

to valued Chinese practices such as guanxi and facework as well as
acceptable to Western business.

> *... for any society to continue to exist over the long run, it must
> solve the problems of how to pass on its total cultural heritage –
> all the ideas, values, attitudes, behavior patterns, and so on – to
> succeeding generations. Should that complexity of cultural
> traditions not be passed on to future generations, it is not very
> likely that the society will survive. (Ferraro, 1998:4)*

If Ferraro is right, what does it take for two very different cultures, joining
together in the 'society of business', to hold hands, and come together to co-
create a shared future? This is a question that foreign invested enterprises
need to ask themselves as they embark on the journey of installing their
businesses in one of the most potentially lucrative (or equally potentially
ruinous) markets in the history of business, that is the China market. The
question is particularly relevant to those who are unaware that the days of
viewing the business world through the eyes of cultures that fostered the
industrial ethic (typically Western eyes), may be coming to an end. We have
the feeling, as we write this book, that history is being made as two powerful
cultures, one industrially powerful and one demographically powerful,
integrate business and cultural activities in the wider sense. In his book
"Understanding China's Economy" Gregory Chow observes *"The
transformation of the economy of the People's Republic of China from a
planned to a more market economy is one of the most significant
developments in world history during the last quarter of the 20th century"*
(Chow, 1994:7)

Daniel H. Rosen writing from an economics perspective, suggests that

> *In the final years of the twentieth century, the United States has little
> choice but to formulate more practical and effective foreign and
> commercial policies towards the People's Republic of China. This
> imperative is made necessary by great economic, political and social
> changes taking place in recent years. To succeed, the architects of this new
> strategy will need an accurate and nuanced understanding of today's
> China (Rosen, 1999:1)*

It is plausible to assume that what goes for the U.S. goes for much of the Western world in this regard. This is because, as Ferraro (1998:4) makes clear, sociological and psychological theories (including theories of work and business) are concentrated on people from Western societies. Inevitably, organizational designers are likely to construct theories based on Western assumptions of 'reality'. Now, however, as the importance of the China business setting to the expatriate business world increases, there is a need to make way for other assumptions. To find the Chinese heartbeat, business people, when developing strategies, need to enter the Chinese world in a way that the nuances of the Chinese way of thinking can be taken into account.

The need to understand the Chinese psyche is seen to be imperative from the standpoint of economic strategy and especially important for those developing strategies for managing the human resource. During our exposure to many managers and senior managers, both expatriate and Chinese, we are coming to the conclusion that whilst a new era is dawning, challenges and opportunities are currently being either unrecognized or somewhat ignored.

The development of industrialization has, as we see later, happened within the wider context of Western civilization. All civilizations interpret their own phenomena through a certain pair of eyes. The meaning of something as simple as a recruitment advertisement may have different symbolism in the impersonal West than it does in the more personal Chinese culture. Consider this observation of an American Chief Executive Officer (CEO), contributed by Rosen

> *In the Western model, he [the CEO] suggested, a business opportunity evolves from identification of what is permissible (legally), to the most logical manner to pursue that end, and finally to the question of what partners need be recruited to accomplish it. In the Chinese marketplace he argued, the sequence is reversed. One takes stock of the assets and trust provided within one's relationships, then asks what opportunities could logically be pursued given these assets and only then are the lawyers sent to find a legal loophole that will permit their pursuit (Rosen, 1999:45).*

It goes without saying that in the universalistic West, the search for a legal loophole might symbolize something different than in the particularistic Chinese setting (Trompenaars, 1998). As Trompenaars says, looking at culture is like peeling onion layers. Each action or event leads down one layer to the deeper meaning to which it can be attributed. Yet we see time and time again, that distinctly Western symbols represented in human resource methodologies, and Western methods are often superimposed upon distinctly Chinese contexts. This is as though first, they had some meaning, and then they had some endemic property of cultural transformation.

Chin (1995:27) researched some of the characteristics of Western versus Chinese (Confucian) ideologies. He referred to Weber, the sociologist (in Gerth & Mills, 1946) as he talked about the Protestant ethic which placed the human in a direct link with God, giving him *"a sense of dignity of the individual thus bringing forth an individualism that is commensurate with the rational organization of labor"*. People worked towards their internal and independent measure of conduct or values. They were (willingly) restrained and constrained by universalistic laws, institutions and societal norms that helped protect individuals from the extravagances of each others' actions. An ingrained responsibility was for each individual to exert as much control over the environment as possible.

People considered the physical and social environment as material ready to be fashioned at will but according to norms of rights and obligations. Assumed in this ethic was the recognition that relationships might be of a transient nature. People had no responsibility to maintain relationships other than in an individually chosen way. Weber contrasted this to the Confucian ethic that tended to encourage people to adapt to the environment. This environment was construed as largely social, not always well defined, and full of Ren or human heartedness. There was the freedom to be vague, as changing and fluid as nature, as long as Li, the social path to the attainment (with honour) of Ren was followed. Far from internal, independent, individual measures of conduct, Confucians valued external, (social) interdependent, group goals of harmony with norms of social responsibility and behavioral ritual (Scarborough, 1998).

Social ritual in Confucianism was all-encompassing across a range of social and status boundaries. It was societal and the social patterns of behavior were taught from birth. They were implicitly yet strongly codified and teaching them was part of a family's obligation. An interesting misconception about Chinese culture is that rationality is missing. Yi, which roughly translates as governing principle, is the method for the adaptation of Li to fit emerging circumstances (McGreal, 1995). Embedded in 'propriety', proper moral character (Lin, 1939) is rational behavior that is geared towards the achievement of a peaceful well-ordered society.

Within the Western ethic, in contrast, the focus was on individual learning. Education was largely academic, that is taught in the classroom. Lessons had subjects and these were typically scientific. This learning, because it was mainly precise and factual, would be assessed and measured objectively and individually. Producing 'evidence' of learning and using the evidence to comment on the ability of individuals was embedded as a social norm and was accepted throughout society. The 'concrete evidence' mindset transferred itself to the organizational setting, especially during the industrial revolution, which saw the development of business methods as we know them today. In line with the traditions of upholding individual rights, organizations would legally define, defend and promote the rights of the individual. They would allow for self-interest and competitiveness to be identified and rewarded. Individual energy would be expended in the pursuit of individual performance. Performance targets would be concrete and specific, as would their measurement.

For the individual in the Chinese ethic, the organizational context would be designed so that the individual role was somewhat subsumed in a set of social relationships. Personal discipline, altruistic consideration for others, energetic cultivation of lasting relationships would be not a matter of personal preference but social expectation. The ritual learning of 'correct' behaviors by managers and employees would be central to an organization's corporate intelligence. In a collective society, an individual's inner energy would be at the service of colleagues and friends, and s/he would expect the same in reverse. We will discuss this point as the book unfolds, however an interesting notion to bear in mind here is the collective versus individual intelligence that can be harnessed for use in the Chinese setting (figures 3 and 4).

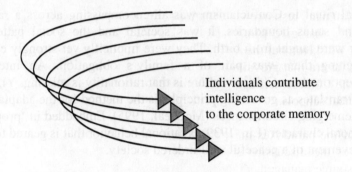

Individuals contribute
intelligence
to the corporate memory

Figure 3. Individual energy for performance

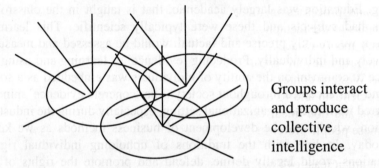

Groups interact
and produce
collective
intelligence

Figure 4. Collective intelligence

Collective intelligence is difficult to achieve in the West, especially across performance levels. The thought structure of the individual, even as a team member is not well matched with the Chinese collective persona. Systemic and deep differences in the things that make people comfortable and want to give of their best need to be addressed by the cross cultural human resource manager. The environment has to be right for people to want to give.

Notwithstanding the need to co-create a suitable environment, we need to be aware that effective human resource management and strategies need to reflect the culture in which they are practiced. This means that the proposed newly constructed reality that somehow brings two philosophies together needs to be true to Chinese rules for propriety and social well being. Rarely do management texts converse at the philosophical level but in the

man resource management, people are a product of the
that give life its generative and evolutionary sustenance. In
sketch out the heritage of the West, paying specific attention to
era that prevailed up to and after the industrial revolution. We
Chinese heritage focussing on Confucianism and other Chinese
philosophical schools.

One of the paradoxes of writing about human resource management in
the light of the discussion so far is that because the formal language of
human resource management systems was developed in the West, there is no
alternative but to conduct much of the conversation about structures,
systems, and processes in these terms. However, as the last chapter will
show, thanks to the metaphorical language offered by chaos (Gleick, 1996),
complexity theory (Stacey, 1998), and complex adaptive systems (Holland,
1995), opportunities are presenting themselves for more figurative thinking
about the Western context. These allow us to escape from the orthodoxy of
Western scientism and to employ a language that could encompass some of
the holistic and non-linear concepts that have stood the test of time in the
way Chinese people prefer to organize themselves.

There are at least two perspectives possible in writing this book – a book
which seeks to faithfully represent the thoughts and observations of people
managing in China, at the same time as trying to make sense of what may
happen in the future. One is to point to the assumed fusion of Western
methodologies with Chinese ones. This would need to be prefaced by
cultural synergy that is conspicuous by its absence. A second is to point out
that Chinese managers and workers feel more or less uneasy with the
imposition of Western methodologies: either they can be partly digested, the
rest spit out or they can be ostensibly adopted whilst the 'real'
methodologies continue under the surface. In either case the real problem of
harmonizing two incompatible cultures is avoided in favor of having one
'official' culture and one 'real' one.

As a result of our extensive involvement with workers and managers,
particularly managers in Hong Kong and other parts of China, we have come
to think that just as the Confucian ethic and the Protestant ethic were
produced as visions of how life should be conducted many centuries ago, a
new business ethic is required but, importantly, one that fits the culture in

which it is practised. Following this theme, as we present data from our research and the literature in future chapters, we will consider the concepts behind the human resource management systems, how they are expressed in Western literature, and what this means to the people managing human beings in Chinese organizations.

2.   Ideology in Context

Western ideology: the business inheritance

> *Theories should be understood as tools for moving from one observation to another. Their sole value lies in their predictive power; and they have this power by virtue of the logical relations which take us from observation to theory and back again. We do not need to suppose that the terms of the theory refer to anything. All that matters is that the predictions come out true. (Scruton, 1997: 191)*

Ideology is the search for clarifying universal ideas and typologies so that the 'chaos' of life can be ordered and understood in terms of unifying and governing principles. There are written, sequential accounts of Western ideologies as they developed through the ages. This makes it a little easier (for the Westerner) to develop a sense of how the Western psyche evolved. Basically, in the West (as everywhere), philosophers sought to work out the nature of virtue and wisdom. They were interested in authentic reality. They were also interested in aspects of it that could give guidance on how people could live in such a way as to ensure morally desirable qualities. These included justice and fairness, good as opposed to evil acts and, based on this, ways of discerning correct as opposed to incorrect behaviors.

Although Western thinking was recorded many years before, it is useful to compare Western and Chinese philosophy from about the same time - that is the time of Confucius. Philosophical thought at this stage was concerned with ideas that very much related to the individual's role in the universal scheme of things. The minds of early philosophers were concerned with many issues including whether mysticism and science should be separately conceived, the notion of skepticism, the need for analysis and logic, the hegemony of thought over the senses (or vice versa), and arguments concerning the existence of an absolute, universal essence (Tarnas, 1991). There was an enormous power in the thinking of time in the West, (not unlike the thought of the Confucian era). Subsequent arguments, rebuttals and extensions of early thought about the hegemony of science over soul and things spiritual have hardly dented the power of scientific thinking about mankind. Even though almost all societies in the West construe good and bad, right and wrong, very differently (Trompenaars, 1998) history has produced a bedrock of thinking about the way Westerners picture themselves.

Although it is only possible in this book to convey a trace of this historical thinking, we can benefit from looking at some of the people whose thinking and concepts have stood the test of time. Tarnas (1991) describes the theories of Socrates (who was an individualist and skeptic), of disbelieving and questioning everything until it was 'proved'. Socrates developed a method for arriving at truth and in his way was as enduring as Confucius (and as unusual in that he did not leave a written record, his work being depicted in Plato's dialogues). Central to Socrates' philosophy was selfhood, self control, self awareness and self reflection. Socrates believed in moral character and the essence of goodness. He also believed that goodness could be and should be rationally moral. Here was the seed of the penchant for categorizing (all virtuous acts), classifying (their qualities) and specifying (through dialectical analysis) words to describe the elements of truth. For Socrates and many that followed him, the process of critical questioning, arguing and debating to find ever more accurate and proven statements was paramount.

Plato followed this tradition with some difference. Plato dealt with those aspects of life that could not be characterized or explained (such as beauty) and sent them off into a transcendental realm where archetypes or eternal ideas representing the 'absolute' truth were located. Through using critical and skeptical analysis, as well as dialectic, the 'insight' to find these absolutes would be gained. This left the world of 'reality' unsullied and the way open for logical coherence and meaningful, true definitions, leading the way for philosophers such as Aristotle (Tarnas, 1991) to articulate

> '*the structure of rational discourse so the human mind might apprehend the world with the greatest degree of conceptual precision...Deduction, and induction, the syllogism, the analysis of causation into material, efficient, formal and final causes, basic distinctions such as subject-predicate, essential-accidental, matter-form, potential-actual, universal-particular genus-species-individual, the ten categories of substance, quality, quantity, relations, place, time, position state, action, affection were all defined by Aristotle and established thereafter as indispensable instruments of analysis for the Western mind*". (*Tarnas, 1991:60*)

Intervening, sometimes with great success, in promoting the spirit and soul (in the form of religion) as the pathway to the true meaning of life, was what we might call the Christian vision. Here mankind was subject to God's will, God's intervention and God's authority (especially where the prevailing view was that man was evil). A soul and mind duality was to characterize Western philosophy in many different ways over the ages. Sometimes the Christian religion dominated thinking and the soul was preeminent. However in our modern era science has somewhat won out, certainly in the case of business life.

The coming of the modern era following the scientific revolution (around the fifteenth century) consolidated many Aristotelian notions, at the same time dispensing with the speculative 'potentiality' components. Mathematicians like Descartes who believed that the world was a 'supreme machine', and scientists like Newton who explained the world through physical laws seemed to put the final seal on the use of science to explain life.

Contaminated as little as possible by human imagination and experience, it was thought that empirical observation, the willingness to doubt everything that could not be observed, and the tools and methods of science, were so efficient and effective that they could be used fruitfully to enlighten individual liberty and rationality, and ultimately, to unlock life's truths.

Some of the world's greatest thinkers in the eighteenth and nineteenth centuries, (represented by the term 'Romantics') sought to introduce the essence of spirit into the precise and unimaginative scientific view. Artistry, emotions, creativity, individual self expression and self creation were seen to operate in a world that did and should have mysteries, moods and unobservable insights. The Romantics introduced the feeling element into philosophical thought, alongside thinking, human will, and a recognition of the indeterminate. Still, as we see today, one has become almost embedded in the other. There is evidence that imagination, self expression and creativity are accepted and even welcomed into the business framework. However, these still seem to be placed in rational and coherent settings.

More recently have emerged the postmodernists. This group could very well be called antimodernists. The postmodernist writers are almost the polar opposite of those who think that imposed rational and functional structures of thought and action are acceptable. Some see the need to deconstruct language and other activities, taking away boundaries that come with definitions, societal norms, defined patterns of behavior and institutionalized practices.

From paradigms to theories and theories to tools and techniques, postmodernists feel that a stranglehold of artificial devices are held in place with the aim of perpetuating the status quo. In postmodernism, the extreme of the rational, logical, structured, and processed world is refuted. The idea is to try and uncover societal devices, examine them for artifice, and to dispense with the terms and institutions that give such devices their power.

If the gamut of Western thinking has gone from one extreme to the other, is there any point in relating some of this ideology to such a practical and contemporary subject as human resource strategies? The answer is undoubtedly "yes". The business setting has some characteristics that can be traced back so far that they have become powerfully assimilated into everyday business life. In the same way, guiding principles in the wider society have prescribed universal 'laws' that tell us how to behave so as not to be deviant and out of the norm. A most important point to bear in mind as we look at excerpts from Western thinking, is that behaving in the way approved and handed down through the generations makes us comfortable, puts us in 'harmony' rather than conflict with ourselves, and frees us to express our individuality in ways that also suit the people around us at work. This feeling of comfort encourages foreign enterprises to design relationships according to their (Western) principles and encourages Chinese recipients to redesign them according to tolerances within the bounds of Chinese norms.

So what makes Western people comfortable? Since the early days of Socrates, people have found comfort in being free to argue, debate, analyze and 'prove' things either scientifically or spiritually. Reason and logic have been themes running through Western development. The notion of a strenuous development and exercise of intellect was accompanied by the notion of a free will. At times this has been connected to a union with some sort of spiritual god, at times rejecting any supernatural being, but the notion of free will has been a continuous thread. Scruton (1997:27) discusses Western reductionists and gives the example of British politician Margaret Thatcher who "notoriously said there is *no such thing* as society, meaning that society is comprised of individuals and nothing else". Throughout the development of Western philosophy, the "I" dominates as the subject/object of which truth is sought. An example is Descartes' famous (though ironic) saying "I think therefore I am". Another is Wittgenstein's ideas on language – that we learn the words for sensation in a way that allows their privileged first person (in Scruton, [1997:51]). Both these examples embody the personal and individual privacy that seems to be the backbone of Western ideology.

The heritage of Western philosophy, therefore, is embedded in the ways foreign enterprises think, feel and act. By nature of the substantial resources and a long term view required to make a success of investing, even with attractive cost and taxation breaks, most foreign invested enterprises will be large and have a history. Some will be the "fashion-setters" (Abrahamson, 1996:255) of commerce and industry, shaping the demand for values, competitive strategies, management styles and techniques. In short, they have often created an 'in' way of doing things. Socio-psychological as well as technical and economic forces will have influenced a paradigm or mental model of how business and management should work for them. It is likely that, over the years, ideas and experiences have produced comprehensive and sophisticated management systems based upon strong beliefs about what is progressive and competitive.

How has management ideology developed? Barley & Kunda (1992) suggest that the journey towards an acceptable management ideology has been painfully gained, starting with the efficiency phase (Taylor, 1929) where the engineering metaphor governed human resource systems and processes. Under this paradigm, time and motion studies aimed to encourage the worker to move faster or better according to efficiency imperatives. In the Human Relations phase between 1925 and 1955 (Mayo, 1930), it was recognized that humans at work were social beings. Group social interaction was to be managed (Lewin, 1951), as well as personal self actualization (Maslow, 1954; Rogers, 1961). The 'self' in organizations became a cornerstone of Western management ideology. Social dynamics were approached from the perspective of how individuals might work and be managed in groups whilst still considered as individual utilities.

The notion that employees were rational and instrumentally motivated (Simon, 1960) fitted nicely with the upsurge in analytical activities aided by the advent of mainframe and then personal computers. Job analysis, job descriptions, job evaluation, and management by objectives (MBO) (Drucker, 1954) became seductive targets for burgeoning statistical and calculative techniques. This era, lasting until the beginning of the 1980's, was significant in laying the traditions of human resource management activities. Indeed, formal, functional and measurable activities are the hallmark of many multinational organizations, including FIEs in China.

Recently, the notion of systems rationalism has been challenged in favor of a more comprehensive cultural view of organizations (Schein, 1993). From this perspective, organizations should be viewed as socially constructed systems of meaning (Pascale, 1990; Pettigrew, 1989; Pondy, 1983). Corporate culture and commitment to quality (within the Western quality movement framework) are current considerations in the human resource arrangements likely to be requested in any invested company.

Barley and Kunda (1992) also suggest that the 'culture' ideology involved engaging employees in commitment to the organization's welfare. Kanter (1984) says of employees in strong cultures that they develop a sense of community. Whiteley (1995) suggests that a forging of individual, group and organizational identities is necessary for a commitment to shared values. It is likely, given the sophisticated and evolved nature of organizational and human resource development in the West that FIEs will be seeking to install the same sort of sophisticated cultural systems in their foreign invested organizations. This is notwithstanding the views of cultural anthropologists that societies (in this case China) have an overriding urge and commitment to pass on a total cultural heritage which in this case could not be further from the Western business heritage. The almost automatic alignment of human resource management strategies and practices with business strategies (Miles & Snow, 1984; Schuler, 1989; Tang, et al., 1996; Walker, 1992) and the inclusion of people at all levels of the organization in human resource and business decisions is one example of such a Western methodology and heritage.

Sweeney (1996) reflects the view held by many expatriate writers that the host country will need to adopt Western ways. Sweeney quotes Child's (1990) employers' assessment of the Chinese workforce, questioning motivation, level of commitment, initiative, loyalty and stamina. He goes on to say that "if Chinese organizations in IBVs are to survive they may need to undergo fundamental cultural change" (Sweeney, 1996:901). This notion has faintly colonial overtones and is a debatable issue as far as this book is concerned. Writers on culture agree that as culture develops, the basic assumptions forge taken-for-granted patterns of behavior (Deal, 1982; Schein, 1985; Frost, 1991). FIEs, unconsciously interpreting the world through the Western cultural lens, will have ascribed a particular meaning to concepts such as loyalty, commitment, motivation, (Barley et al., 1992). These same concepts, attached to bedrock reference points in the Chinese culture such as Confucianism, will conjure up an entirely different set of governing principles. Even the notion of 'the individual self' in organizations, would be expressed differently in the Chinese setting (Han, 1992).

China may be attractive in terms of the size of its market and its increasing willingness since 1978 to open its doors to foreign investment. However, the idea of submitting to what might appear to be management colonization would not be so appealing to the Chinese community. In fact, recent reports suggest that China is insisting on maintaining control over many strategic areas of foreign investment, including telecommunications, financial services, and agriculture (Callick, 1999).

Cheng et al. (1995:117) notes that " ...the relationship between interested parties, enterprises and government has been nullified; foreign capital entering the Chinese market are gradually becoming the most active executive bodies: and human resource management has got many new characteristics due to the changing economic situation". Cheng points to unsolved human resource problems such as how enterprises can improve the task of attracting labor, external and internal recruitment, but also, importantly, how to integrate human resource strategy in the PRC with the national development policy of China. In other words, human resource arrangements need to fit with broader social and cultural as well as economic developments.

Cheng's concern is clear when she says that "it is self-evident that transnational companies will exercise control and influence on their enterprises in China through the use of their own human resource management mode" (Cheng, et al., 1995:119). Such a view is valid when one considers that the nearly a third of the world's largest transnational companies are investing in the PRC, many of them spanning several provinces. Even though those who are successfully employed in FIEs might be temporarily happy (research in Singapore [International Survey Research Corporation, 1996] showed that 73% of 5,625 employees surveyed were happy in work relationships, 64% were happy with employee involvement, and 60% were happy with supervision), emergent issues could well be predicted. For example, the same study showed that social and organizational ills such as wages drift (67% felt underpaid) and pressure (59% felt pressured) were incipient problems. Writers such as Cheng have signaled that these issues are out of step with wages and work practices in other sectors, including the influential State-owned enterprise sector.

Chinese Ideology

> *A Chinese story relates that once a man met an immortal who asked him what he wanted. The man said that he wanted gold. The immortal touched several pieces of stone with his finger and they immediately turned to gold. The immortal asked the man to take them but he refused. "What else do you want?" the immortal asked. "I want your finger" the man replied. The analytic method is the finger of the Western philosophers and the Chinese want the finger (Fung, 1948/1997).*

China's size is enormous, with 3.7 million square miles scattered across lowlands and highlands, mountains and plains (De Mente, 1990). Of this, only a fraction is habitable, rendering China still land-hungry and people rich. China has over fifty ethnic races living in over twenty provinces and several autonomous or special administrative regions. They are joined by one written language system, but separated by many spoken languages. Although China is often associated with its key cities, its culture, its unique recipe for survival and success was predicated on the agricultural model. For over four thousand years it has perfected farming under varying conditions. For the past few decades, China has used technology and updated methods to advance industrial as well as farming development.

There is a need to consider the underlying culture of China even when it embraces the latest technological and technical systems. China is a country that has one of the oldest and most classical civilizations in the world. It has developed continuously and to understand the contemporary context for employee relations and human resource management in the PRC and Hong Kong it is necessary to bear the history of China in mind.

When conversing with Chinese people, either in China or overseas, the cultural heritage most often referred to is that of Confucius, the Chinese philosopher and teacher. At a time when up to 98% of the country was illiterate and the scholar or *Jinshr* was a revered font of knowledge and authority, Confucius developed a set of teachings based on "...absolute respect for tradition on a carefully ranked hierarchy founded on primary relationships between members of families and between the people and their rulers" (De Mente, 1990:19). Confucius seems to have embodied the accepted rules of behavior and values that people of China could translate into everyday life. A scholar at a time when scholars and their opinions were revered and taken as law, Confucius was willing and able to travel amongst ordinary people with his 'formulas' for an appropriate conduct that was suitable to shape and sustain the foundations of Chinese society.

The major ideas of Confucius (McGreal, 1995) were *Ren* or human heartedness as the highest virtue, *Li*, social norms, obligations and behavioral ritual (to be regulated by methods such as the rectification of names, in which the name represents an actuality which then has to be enacted) and education with the goal of furthering an ordered and peaceful society. Interestingly, in our current work on Chinese leadership (Wood, Whiteley, & Zhang, 1999), asking leaders what their subordinates expected in a leader, the answers could well have embodied almost all of these Confucian qualities.

McGreal (1995), gives us some definitions centered around the concept of *Ren*, a natural and humanistic love for humankind (figure 1).

Xiao

is filial piety, the cultivated respect for one's parents

Di

is brotherly love

Junzi

is a superior, cultivated or perfect person

Ren

Zhong

is loyalty to superiors, employers or country

Yi

is the proper character that allows one to speak in the right way at the right time in the right place

Li

means rituals, rites and propriety, the way one's cultivated feelings can be expressed

Figure 1. The concept of Ren

Adapted from McGreal, I. *Great thinkers of the eastern world: The major thinkers and the philosophical and religious classics of China, India, Japan, Korea and the world of Islam*. New York: Harper Collins, page 4, 1995.

Confucius' emphasis was on form and function, prescribed virtues and self-monitored morality (Chu, 1973). Whether it was his accessibility, acceptability or a combination of both, it seems as though he was able to lay down a 'right' way to conduct relationships. Softened by later scholars, such as Mencius and Hsi Chu, his dictates became humanized and woven into the fabric of Chinese culture (Fung, 1948/1997). Contemporary writers on Chinese culture, (Bond, 1986; Lasserre, 1995) agree that notwithstanding the lure of the West and of such modern influences as consumerism, the Confucian ethic remains the bedrock of Chinese thought and behavior (Yau, 1988).

Although Confucius dominated Chinese philosophy, scholars before and after him were also influential, particularly in keeping the legends alive, albeit with (sometimes very) different emphases. Lao Tzu, for example, introduced the idea of yielding to the primordial ways of the universe. Things that were indefinable had no definite name, but the idea was embodied in the concept of Dao or Tao, the 'way'. There was a 'way' to do everything. Some Tao tenets are clearly challenging to Confucianism, especially the idea of spontaneity and emergence (*Wuwei*) versus deliberation and order.

According to Lao Tzu, natural emergence of things is more important than sophistication. Being open, or "uncarved" leads to leaving options open, the more carving (or sophistication) the less left to see. Seeing things, even (or especially) opposites, as complementary and part of each other and recognizing the law of reversal, (the nearer a thing is to its extreme, the nearer it is to becoming its opposite), is central to the Tao. These ideas add a softness, fluidity, flexibility and reversibility to the more fixed Confucian way of thinking. A most important symbolic aspect of the Tao is the mystical Yin and Yang. This is an intriguing concept, emphasizing as it does the 'each is in the other' - the dark, soft, feminine, recessive and contractive side found in the light, hard, dominant, masculine, solid and expansive side.

Later scholars added their own distinctive stamp to Chinese ideology. Mozi (Mo Tzu) followed Confucius, sharing the same ends but disagreeing on the means to achieve them. Mo's followers, (the Mohists) sought to achieve human relatedness through inner perfection. They repudiated vain habits, advocated frugality and austerity and valued benevolence and mutual sharing. A tension developed between self interest and altruism with Mencius adding the dimension of a 'theory of moral human nature' (humankind is essentially good and virtuous and moral virtues are innate, a set of potentials waiting to develop, through, for example, the ways laid down by Confucius). In contrast, Xunzi (Hsün Tzu) (McGreal, 1995) believed that human nature was evil, although humans could acquire goodness - any man can become a sage. Standards of goodness were to be developed and passed on from rulers to subjects, teachers to students, parents to children and so on down the line.

From Confucius was handed down the idea of correct behaviors, rules of conduct, and rituals whilst from Lao Tzu, came the Tao, and laws of nature. In some form or another, these were preserved through the ages right to the time of Tan Sitong (T'an Ssu-T'ung) (McGreal, 1995), around the time that the industrial revolution was happening in the West. At this time Chinese scholars and philosophers were in a transitional age. Traditions were still strong and yet there was a persistent Western influence to be faced. Philosophers like Tan Sitong were concerned that China was backward and needed to be reformed and rejuvenated (McGreal, 1995:134). Themes from Western Christianity such as the love of management were resonant with Chinese philosophies such as that of Mozi, as well as with Buddhist traditions of compassion and unity. In the Western way of thinking, typically one or other of the dominant philosophies of the time would have prevailed. The Chinese way, according to Fung (1948/1997:322) was to synthesize and harmonize schools of thought "Neo-Confucianism is a synthesis of Confucianism, Buddhism, philosophical Taoism (thorough Ch'ianism) and religious Taoism".

This ended the era of the classical Chinese philosophy to some extent and a 'new age' of the competing and primarily political reforms of Sun Yat-sen and Mao Zedong arrived (McGreal, 1995).

Each brought a different political view to the Chinese situation - Sun Yatsen's being a particular brand of democracy and Mao Zedong's being a brand of communism. It is beyond the scope of this book to enter into comparisons and contrasts. However, we could think of each as a different blueprint for bringing more of the proletariat into the national decision making and economic structures, as well as planning for the industrialization of China. In the case of Taiwan, this was achieved by integration with Western industrial influences.

An important difference in the industrial development of China is the way it developed as other nations were experiencing the Industrial Revolution and with it scientific management (Taylor 1929, Weisbord, 1987). Having dipped in and out of experiments in opening itself up to trade and relationships with other countries, China seemed to emerge with an even firmer resolve to close itself off from the outside (industrial) world. China was internally focussed for a large part of the industrial era. Unlike Hong

Kong, which had available the talents and resources of developed countries as well an unremitting sense of trade and business, China did not experience business in the Western sense at the time of, and for some time after, the industrial revolution. It concentrated, instead, on developing the communist ideology, and with it very different cultural patterns for living in an exclusive way. As the adapted model from Yau (1988) suggests, this way involved very different values from the rational, scientific, analytical, 'here and now', independent and individualistic West. As Scarborough (1998) points out, Chinese traits are more intuitive, and implicit, aesthetic, synthetic, patient, dependent and group oriented. Figure 2 below captures some of the values inherent in Chinese relations (Yau, 1988).

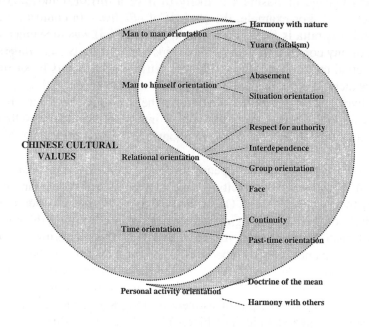

Figure 2. Chinese relational values

Source: Adapted from Yau, O. Chinese Cultural Values: Their Dimensions and Marketing Implications. *European Journal of Marketing* 22(5), page 46, 1988.

The period since China began to open its doors to trade and investment is a relatively short one, compared with its history of closed doors and reluctant international activity. Deeply ingrained custom is never far from the surface, including the customs of hospitality, 'making a good impression', ritualized etiquette, and enthusiasm in demonstrating cultural accomplishments. This should signal to the business person in China that there is a strong, if not always observable undercurrent of shared understanding about the place and role of business in the Chinese psyche. This understanding may not be the same as that of other countries, for many of whom business is almost a national culture.

The language of business is likely to have a different meaning in the Chinese world. For example, the concept of *efficiency* in countries like the USA and Australia is finely honed, linked to time and resources and almost devoid of any connection with relationships unless these are an integral part of the actual task at hand. In the Chinese setting, *efficiency* is likely to be of the bureaucratic type, mediated by officials and at the same time including any networking opportunities that might help present or future business activities. Traits that are particularly important in Human Resource Management are those concerning relationships.

However since China has opened its doors, some important changes have occurred. This is a very exciting time in the history of human resource strategy theory development. On the one hand, the Western world is eager to avail itself of the burgeoning consumer market in China, the relatively low costs of manufacturing and the attractive Government terms for foreign invested companies. On the other hand, there will continue to be an impact, possibly stronger than any so far in the industrial history of the West, of the Chinese character. With regards to FIEs, it seems evident that although at present some of the 'foreign' investment is Hong Kong, Taiwan and Macau, (all to some degree technically Chinese) based, further influence will come from industrially developed Western multinationals.

As well as considering the strategies and tactics necessary to enhance performance in China it is, we feel, necessary to consider China's history and current social economic challenges. These issues affect human resource issues for managers in, or coming in to work in the Chinese setting. In the remainder of this chapter, Zhang Shiquan from the International Technology

Economy Institute (ITEI) Development Research Center of the State Council, People's Republic of China, writing from Beijing, describes the social and economic setting within which study of human resource management in China is framed. The more historical setting described in chapter one is a reminder that although China has recently 'opened its door', it has a rich and pervasive cultural heritage which human resource managers need to be able to incorporate into human resource strategies and practices.

The economic context

As an initial picture of the Chinese setting, we will now present the current economic situation in China with statistics on the labor force, living conditions, educational levels, geographical distribution of people. We will then discuss what this information means for those trying to develop social and economic macro policies in China. We will also discuss some of the new initiatives launched by the Chinese government and the problems associated with the most recent employment legislation.

Accompanying the waves of international economy unification and system reform, the 1997 Hong Kong hand-over and the 15th National Congress of the Communist Party of China marked China's accelerating transition to interface with the world economy through a market economy system. In the years 1996 and 1997, the strengthening of macro-economic control has greatly improved the power of the nation. When certain problems threatening the smooth operation of the economy were resolved, people started to focus their attention on implementing checks and balances in order to tackle the deeper problem of maintaining healthy social and economic development in the long run. Major human resource management challenges, discussed later, are amongst the areas for the checks and balances to be made.

1996 – 98 Macro-economy development indices and some of the problems

During this period, China's economic, financial, monetary, internal and external trade activities functioned smoothly. An outstanding characteristic of its economic operation was the ability to maintain low inflation under rapid economic growth. According to information published by the State Statistical Bureau in 1998, retail product prices increased by 0.8% during 1997, down 5.3% from the 6.1% in 1996, the lowest increase for over 5 years. Table 1 compares the GDP figures of 1992 through 1997.

Year	Gross Domestic Product
1992	26638.1
1993	34634.4
1994	46759.4
1995	58478.1
1996	67884.6
1997	74772.4

Table 1. China's GDP 1992-1997

Source: China Statistical Yearbook (1998)

GDP increased 10.1% between 1996 and 1997. Over 10% growth in one year is a rate that tops the world, thus attracting international attentions. The rapid economic growth in China has raised its international position. However, the associated problem is whether different areas of the national economy can keep on sustaining such a high growth rate. Coordinated development is therefore of paramount importance. Current problems of structure, construction, and overproduction are discussed later in this book as HRM issues and are connected to the high growth rate.

Peoples' Income: From 1990 to 1997, the overall living standard of people in the cities and villages greatly improved. The average income for living expenses for people in the cities and the per capita net income of people in the villages helps to illustrate this (Tables 2 and 3).

Year	Per capita net income of rural households (yuan)
1990	686.31
1995	1577.74
1996	1926.07
1997	2090.13

Table 2. Per capita net income of rural households 1990-1997

Source: China Statistical Yearbook (1998)

Year	Per capita living expenditure of urban households (yuan)
1990	1278.89
1995	3537.57
1996	3919.47
1997	4185.64

Table 3. Per capita living expenditure of urban households 1990-1997

Excerpt from Comment on Economic Condition (3), People's Daily, 1st August 1997.

If a comparison is made on the average wealth of people with those of developed countries, China would, of course, be placed at the bottom portion of the list regardless of whether the comparison is on per capita output, per capita resources, or per capita income. Furthermore, the big gap between the rich and the poor in China becomes a problem in income distribution. As we see in the 'HRM Challenges' discussion, the income difference between cities and villages is still widening.

During 1992-1997, the growth rate of China's total import and export was higher than that of its GDP. This indicated that China has become one of the prominent countries in world trade. China is now more tied to the world economy and its dependence on worldwide resources and world markets has also increased. In 1995, 40% of China's GDP came from foreign trade. In 1996, it dropped below 36%, rising to slightly over this level in 1997. This decrease in dependency following China's economic development indicates that the economic power of people living in China has increased. This naturally pushed up internal market demand and increased the market share for locally produced products.

FIEs are playing a more important role in import and export trading. During the 14 years between 1983 to 1996, the total amount of import and export business generated by foreign invested enterprises increased at the average rate of 51.7% per year, 3.3 times the average rate of increase in total foreign trade for the entire nation. Between 1996 and 1997 alone, import and export trading generated by foreign invested enterprises increased by over 11%. In addition, in 1995, 31.5% of total export was conducted by foreign invested enterprises; this percentage has increased in 1997 to 41%.

Impacts of The Open Door Policy in China

In 1996, the policies and steps announced by the Chinese Government clearly indicated its continued desire to attract foreign investors, especially multinational companies, to invest directly in China. It also showed that an environment enabling fair competition amongst local and foreign enterprises was in the process of being provided. In 1998, for example, a major priority has been the establishment of a medicare system for city workers, and the implementation of pensions for retirees in all regions. Other policies and steps include further opening up of the China market with a sharp reduction of customs duty, offering equal treatment to local and foreign enterprises, opening the service industry more to foreign investors and opening up of mid-west region of China to outside investment and trade.

As another example, the Department of State made an announcement on 22nd August 1996 stating that provinces, autonomous regions and other designated cities could now directly approve foreign investment projects worth 30 million US dollars or less (up from the original upper limit of 10 million). This was provided that they complied with the "Provisional Regulations on Guiding Foreign Investment Direction" and "Industry Catalogue for Foreign Investment". This meant that there was then no need for external intervention to solicit local investment, or to provide infrastructure and facilities. Regions could carry out production and operation, and acquired foreign exchange on their own. This new policy attempted to propel provinces and cities to put more focus on utilizing foreign investment.

Up to now, China has opened up 359 cities and counties, more than 300 million people, and over 500 000 square miles of land to outside investors. Those areas opened up earlier in time are developing at an extremely fast pace. The coastal cities and provinces are an example. These cities and provinces represent 58% of the nation's GDP; absorb approximately 88% of foreign investments in the entire nation and contribute to 89% of the national's total imports and exports. Their average economic growth rate is twice that of the entire nation. This is especially true for the Special Economic Zones along the coast that continuously show a 30% growth rate. (Estimation based on 1997 China Statistics Summary)

Up to 1997, China had approved the setting up of a total of over 290 000 foreign investment enterprises, over 80% of which were approved during or after 1992. Certain industries are also opening up their doors to outside investors. For example, approval was given to various financial institutes to open up a total of 540 representative offices in China and 162 financial organizations that can conduct trading in China. Recently, foreign banking institutes in PoTung were given approval to conduct local currency related businesses. The total capital investment from such foreign banking institutes has already reached US$33 billion.

For four consecutive years from 1993 to 1996, China attracted the second highest amount, after the US, of foreign investments. China takes up 40% of the 100 billion US dollars per year of direct investment made to developing countries around the world.

The following characteristics have emerged during the recent 2 years:

- The scale of projects has expanded and investment structure has improved. In 1996 the average size of single project investment reached US$3 million compared to only US$1 million before 1992. Currently, most of the projects are medium, or large scale, with a long life cycle. Taking the Zu Zhou Industrial City District as an example, it has the biggest single project investment worth over US$30 million. This demonstrates the increasing penetration of foreign investors into China's economy.
- Sources of investment have diversified and the number of regions opened up for investment have expanded. Up to the end of June 1997, over 170 countries and regions around the world had invested in China and the regions for investment had expanded from coastal to inner parts of China.
- Increasing investment from multinational companies has created an internal market between the investing enterprises and their parent companies. Currently, over 200 of the 500 prominent multinational companies have already made their investment in China, establishing factories and a business presence. Many used different investment channels, thus establishing many individual enterprises. For example, 36 enterprises alone have been established by Siemens since 1982 (Bjorkman & Lu, 1999). Such enterprises have huge investment power, high quality skills, advanced technologies, and stringent management. Therefore, they play an important role in pushing changes in the style of foreign investment in China from a quantitative to a qualitative one.

Currently, foreign invested enterprises employ over 17 million people in China. Based on the various performance indices for the last 5 years, FIEs will have an increasing impact on the overall economic structure of China. These indices include: speed of development; annual gross production v/s national GDP increase ratio, and contribution to increased national import and export business. In 1995 alone, 14.5% of China's gross industrial product came from foreign invested enterprises. China possesses both cheap production resources (although these are gradually disappearing in coastal regions) and huge market potential. This, together with the non-stop growth during the transition to a market economy has attracted a lot of foreign investors. The advanced skills and technologies, new management and sales systems offered by these foreign investment enterprises have contributed greatly to China's growing GDP. It is undeniable that China has benefited greatly from the introduction and practical operations of foreign investment.

However, it is the power of foreign investors, rather than the power of the national economy that is expanding at an unprecedented rate. In businesses with a wide market perspective, high demand for flexibility, and fierce competition, multinational companies use their superiority in advanced skills and technologies to dominate and monopolize the market. To gain control over an enterprise or even a business sector, they demand stock-holding options when seeking local partners. They allow only their joint ventures to use their brand name in order to expand the market share of the parent companies. All these have limited, to a certain extent, the accumulation of capital and the development of local enterprises. They have also restricted the research and development capability of Chinese enterprises as a whole making it difficult for newly developed industries to survive. As a result, although China has achieved a high GDP, the businesses that form China's competitive backbone are fragile. Certain businesses are not even under the nation's own control. Even though the current development of foreign investment activities in China benefits China's economy, there is no doubt that there are threats to local enterprises.

The influence of the Asian financial crisis has also encouraged the Chinese government to adopt a series of measures designed to open China up further to foreign investment. These include revision of the index of guidance for foreign investment, resumption of a curtain of reduction and exemption from taxation for technology imports, and the decision by the State-Council that FIEs established before 1994 and engaged in the trade of processing activities would be relieved of substantial tax burdens.

However, rather than look at this as a conflict, we should view it as a challenge to local enterprises. Such competition should be welcomed as it helps to strengthen survival capability. Furthermore, from a holistic perspective, very few foreign investment enterprises are related to the life-blood businesses of China's national economy. They have yet to achieve leadership positions. There is no need for immediate concern as China's average foreign investment per capita is still relatively low when compared with other countries in South East Asia. However, the situation leads us to ponder about the 'shelf life' of the singularly Western management strategies and practices transported to China. There is no guarantee that, as the Chinese workforce gains both confidence and education, it will not superimpose Chinese methodologies on the Western ones, especially in terms of relations within the workplace.

However such occurrences may be more likely to occur in the future rather than in the immediate present. In the past few years, implementation of radical economic reform has been the main vehicle for achieving economic development. China believes that this is the only way it can face the challenges and problems associated with opening up to the outside world. As discussed below, the main obstacle in sustaining continuous economic development in China is its huge population and low quality of labor. The nation needs to meet this challenge by leveraging its continuous development so that social as well as economic problems can be solved.

The huge population and low quality of labor are two facets of one single problem. The success in population and birth control has greatly reduced the speed of population growth to a predictable number. The next step is to raise the overall quality of the population as a whole and to convert the labor force to become a productive human resource. In the past, China believed that the bottleneck in raising the quality of its people lay in funding. Therefore, it concentrated on fund injection with funding on education reaching 3% of GDP. However, funding does not mean that quality can be sharply increased in a short period of time. It is perhaps better to rally quality improvement initiatives through human resource systems and policies (e.g. enterprise initiatives such as training and development, and external [Government] initiatives such as occupational training to meet market needs). On the positive side, many knowledgeable people are already promoting this concept. Well established enterprises have their own training institutions with the Government recognizing the need for both Government funding and effective human resource allocation. At the micro-level, the foreign invested enterprise structure is leading the way.

Improving the quality of the labor force is fundamental to attracting foreign investment to China. An important condition for multi-national enterprises to move and expand their investment in any country is the country's capability to quickly absorb and master new skills and technologies. The availability of a vast labor force is a favorable condition for labor intensive industries. China tops the world in the amount of labor resource it can offer. Investors from developed countries can thus move some of their production to China. When considering the entire population of China as a whole, the average skill level and quality is low, in terms of absolute numbers. Whilst it is true that there are many highly skilled individuals specializing in various technologies in China, as can be seen in later chapters, these people are aware of their assets as a bargaining tool.

Two major restrictions in raising the quality and standard of the labor resource in China are its size and growing base population. Because of the large base, even a very controlled and slow growth in population represents a big number. The average annual population increase in China during the 1990s is predicted to be 15 million. The total population is expected to reach 1.3 billion by the year 2000 and, when combined with the already vast labor force, this has resulted in increased unemployment.

This result is, however, due to two factors. First, there is the amount of excessive labor force in villages. This has reached 120 million people, representing over one quarter of the total labor force in villages. By the year 2000 this number will reach 200 million, 60% of whom will go to cities to look for jobs. They are called "Min Kung". This in-flux of labor further aggravates the excessive labor problem in the cities. Secondly, with the increasing rate of privatization as China progresses towards a market economy, certain operations face recession. This may be due to a lack of understanding of market demand or simply that these operations belong to sunset industries. A common characteristic of enterprises that are in the red, for example, is stagnant sales. State-owned enterprises are exhibiting over 40% loss and yet employ about a third too many people according to the Chinese Entrepreneur Survey System. Therefore, the 'excess labor' problem that already existed in enterprises becomes ever more serious. It is estimated that excessive labor currently represents 5 – 12% of the total labor force employed by various enterprises. This amounts to approximately 15 million people of which about 11 million are from State-owned enterprises.

However, due to the social responsibility that these State-owned enterprises have historically assumed, it becomes very difficult for them to lay off employees. This results in a conflict between the Government's goal of reducing the unemployment rate and the goal of enterprises to be productive. As things stand at present, FIEs do not have the same problem as State-owned enterprises. Most of their excess personnel are unable to meet the demand for positions in the new enterprises.

This issue is most evident in the lack of high-level management talent and the availability of people who are highly adaptive and possess general skills. Statistics shows that less than 30% of all professionals and managers in the nation have received higher-level education. This brings out a big contradistinction between the current quality of human resources available at this stage in China's economic development and the demand for highly skilled people from multinational companies that invest directly in China. On the other hand, if China is able to make use of the results of its economic development to upgrade the quality of its human resources, it should be able to gain enormous benefits.

Improvement in living standards is the foremost task in upgrading the quality standards of people in China where improvements have been made. However with a generally improved standard of living comes the problem of enlarged wage differentials. Normal causes of wage difference such as capability, work load, company and management operations do not account for such big gaps. The gaps are, in turn, caused by the unbalanced development in different industries and regions.

According to results of studies such as the Wu Shiu Xian Study and the Chinese Entrepreneur Survey System Study, due to higher wages and better advancement opportunities, half of the total number of top employees leaving Chinese enterprises moved to work in FIEs. Most of the other employees moved to work in local private enterprises and organizations. This indicated that Chinese enterprises cannot retain good people. Foreign invested enterprises also attracted a large number of top people using high salaries. How to retain the most important human asset in enterprises has become the most pertinent question, and most needed answer, to Chinese entrepreneurs.

Large differences in income also exist between different regions. In 1997, the average income of a resident in Shanghai was 8 439 RMB while it was 3 945 RMB in Mongolia, a 213% difference. The income difference within a city is also gradually increasing. In 1996, amongst the nearly 150 million working individuals, over 10 million were considered in poverty. Adding their family members to the picture, the number reached 30 million people. These living conditions continue to deteriorate as under-employment and inflation is confronted. Withholding and even the stopping of salary payment is commonly seen. Although minimum living expenses insurance has already been announced in many cities and towns, there are still employees who cannot cover their basic expenses.

The selection of new economic growth locations mainly refers to the combination of certain cities in China and reasonably established industries. The central Government has already formulated plans offering more favorable policies to those cities and industries, such as the basic medical cover of city workers. It is hoped that this will attract foreign investments to the western and northern parts of China.

The Government has learned from the experience of macro-economy control that inflation, uncontrolled expansion of investment activities, together with the non-stop establishment of new businesses, are not sensible ways to relieve employment problems. Instead, they can be tackled through the establishment of a social security system. The creation of programs such as employee re-deployment are needed to help those being laid-off as a result of company merger, bankruptcy, or re-organization. These programs represent important tactics in human resource development under the market economy system. In the past, social security was tied to "the unit" and not to society. This put a very heavy burden on enterprises. Retirement insurance was provided by "one whole plan". Individuals did not need to make any contribution. Once they lost their working capability or retired, they would enjoy insurance as mandated by the Government. All related expenses were borne by the enterprise. This situation was changed in 1996.

The consolidated retirement insurance system joint investigation team was headed by the Labor Department and the National Reform Committee, together with seven unit Committees in the Department of State as members. In August 1996, the Team submitted the "Main Points in the Enterprise Employee Consolidated Retirement Insurance System Report" to the Department of State. They suggested the framework for the retirement Insurance System which was accepted in principle by the Department of State.

The main points included a personal account to be set up based on 11% of an employee's salary. The employee contributed 8% (currently individual contribution is mostly 3% which will be increased at 1% per year), with the company contributing 3% (currently mostly at 8% which will be gradually decreased). Regional Governments were to decide local companies' contribution ratios, which were not to exceed 20% of average salary, and carry out implementation of the system. Payment of pension would be in two portions. The first portion would be the basic pension, following the standard of 25% of local average salary or below and further subdivided based on length of payment. The second portion would be the personal pension fund with a standard monthly payment of 120th of the accumulated saving in the personal pension fund. Three different schemes were being used in different parts of China in 1996. These have since moved to the consolidated system by the 'end of 1998' deadline.

The two social security items that are most conflicting, generate most suggestions from the general public, and require the most coordination work are employee pensions and medical insurance. The fund involved in these two items represents over 90% of the entire social security fund in cities and towns. The most urgent task has been consolidation of the management of these two items. Various departments currently perform this task. The Social Security Department is to consolidate and take over all related work thus eliminating mis-management and restrictions. This will lower the cost of management, reduce the burden on the enterprises, and speed up reform.

Education is the main route to raise national human resource standards. According to statistics, 16% of Chinese over 15 years of age are literate. 420 million have completed primary school education (representing 37% of the entire population) and less than 2% of the entire population has completed post-secondary or higher-level education. Although this is of concern to the Government, the shortage of education funding has often been a big bottleneck. In 1993 for example, the average per capita spending in education in China was US$9. This was much lower than the number one country, Sweden, who spent US$ 2,287 per person. Career training should not be included in the education spending mentioned above. It is argued that enterprises should pay for such training to increase their competitiveness. However, due to lack of capital, such areas cannot be covered by State-owned enterprises. Foreign invested enterprises can and do pay more attention to this area. Therefore they are able to be more competitive and increase their market share.

Fortunately, direct investment made by Chinese investors from Hong Kong, Macau, Taiwan and other parts of the world has had a further positive impact on foreign investment in China. Although the ratio of investments from Hong Kong, Macau and Taiwan has decreased in recent years, investors from these regions still contribute almost 40% of the total foreign investment in China. These investments focus on the labor intensive manufacturing industry, thus helping to resolve employment problems in certain districts and also keep them in touch with the world economy. Therefore, they also enjoy certain favorable policies offered to other foreign investors. Furthermore, people perceive these investments as a special form of Chinese capital, playing an undeniable part in China's development.

China will continue its current foreign investment policies to attract investment from multinational companies. It is the right decision to enable upgrading of industry infrastructure and gain the skills, knowledge and information that are currently lacking in China. The entrance of multinational companies into the Chinese market has raised competition making it difficult for certain local enterprises to survive. However, this also presents the biggest opportunity to those enterprises if they can rise above the competition and utilize foreign investment to (in this order) bring in advanced technologies and skills; bring in advanced management practice; utilize foreign capital and utilize FIEs' sales channels.

Competition is the catalyst to improve quality of enterprises. An important question is whether conditions exist for *fair* competition. Research is still in progress to look into the protection of local enterprise development -- whether certain businesses should be allowed free competition amongst foreign and local enterprises.

In order to enjoy favorable policies from the Chinese Government and maintain a prosperous business future, foreign companies investing in China need to integrate with China's economic development needs thus enabling adjustment in industry infrastructure. As discussed earlier, a core problem arises because of China's huge and relatively low quality labor force. Low quality here refers to employees' lack of capability to adapt to various employment channels. Therefore in less developed districts such as the midwest of China, the most appropriate type of industry to develop is the labor intensive industry.

It is only through engaging in infrastructure development that employment positions can be increased. Multinational companies need to focus more of their investments in advanced technologies. This, on the one hand, helps China in upgrading and re-organizing its industry infrastructure; on the other hand, it also helps to open up new markets. These gains can be further increased by enterprises increasing their efforts in human resource management and particularly employee training and development so as to improve both the quality of labor and also their profit.

The fact that representatives of the Chinese and the U.S. governments signed the bilateral agreement on Chinese entry to the WTO on November 15, 1999 cleared away the largest obstacle for China to enter into the "economic United Nations". Going through the course of reforming and opening up, China has already mixed with the tide of globalization, and has been a part of trade and investment in the world's economy. As the largest developing country, entry to the WTO could promote both world trade development and the establishment of a new economic system, so that China is able to play a larger role in the stable development of the global economy.

With the prerequisite of some degree of national influence, China itself, with its broad market and potential, could absorb more investment from abroad in order to enhance employment and to enable industrial structure and restructure; could show a comparative advantage and promote a Chinese position in the world economy; could, as a member of WTO, use its multilateral conflict system to solve trade issues and, with the principles of non-discrimination and the clause of fair competition could also protect its important interests; and furthermore, could force most Chinese enterprises, in particular, the state-owned enterprises, to take the opportunity of enhanced competiton to enter the international market - without such pressures, these enterprises would not go forward and abroad.

Of course, China could face a lot of challenges after entering the WTO. With clauses concerning trade and investment liberalization, the economic shock that has occurred in other countries could spread to China. The speed of market opening could force national enterprises to go bankrupt if they are unable to cope with competition in such a short lead time. Enterprises could go bankrupt under the pressure of multinational companies entering into China, in which case strategic targets of rising employment and rising income may not be met by WTO membership. Furthermore, the process of globalization and the rules for entering WTO still reflect somewhat, the willpower of developed countries - how to follow WTO's clauses and yet avoid paying too high a cost in terms of national interests, is the challenge China faces in achieving a "double win" in the WTO.

This description of the situation in China makes it important for human resource managers to critically appraise the human resource strategies and practices they transport from abroad, or receive from foreign invested enterprises. There is a dire need, as expressed above, for professional and knowledgeable human resource managers to take existing theory as a base from which to develop something very new. A hybrid of Western and Chinese methodologies is not as good as an attempt to forge a new set of theories. These will cause people from both perspectives to rethink in a way that each sees the world to some extent through the other's eyes. An essential aspect of this is the theoretical models and frameworks upon which human resource strategies and business strategies are expressed. In the next chapter, some of the existing concepts and theories attached to human resource management will be further explained.

3. Human Resources in the Context of Business Strategy

Human Resources in the Context of Business Strategy

The identifying features of the human resource managerial role are considered by management writers (Torrington, 1985; Tyson, 1995), to include:

- Having a position of centrality in the organization, usually conveyed by a presence in the boardroom as a part of the business strategy formulation team;
- Creating, through activities such as the ability to attract, maintain and reward appropriate people for the present and the future;
- Harmonizing the human resource strategy with the business strategy in such a way that a set of integrated functional activities blend to complement each other.
- Promoting consideration of the human resource as an asset rather than a cost; associated with long-term as opposed to short-term strategies;
- Fostering the perception of human resources as necessary to successful business performance (not only through productivity enhancement but through the strategic use of the human as opposed to technical resource);
- Being a major strategist of organizational change and transformation

This definition is attached to the Western orthodoxy. "Typically HRM refers to those functions undertaken by an organization to effectively utilize human resources. These functions would include at least the following: Human resource planning, Staffing, Performance evaluation, Training and development, Compensation, Labor relations, Benefits and in-house communication" (Dowling, 1994:2,3). The linguistic boundary around orthodox human resource management is often functional, even when strategic status is achieved. Connections in human resource management are usually made to in-work issues such as strategies, structures, organizational context and the business environment interface. In the Chinese setting, very often a system-within-a-system is in place where functional language and structures are evident, however these do not always act as boundaries between work and family structures.

The time boundary is an example of work as a separate functional activity. Although there is little doubt that Western people, especially executives, work many hours outside of the contractual time, this is conceptualized as "over-time". In the Chinese setting, people may or may not necessarily work after time but the concept of work often belongs to the whole family rather than the individual. The clear division between work and leisure is also blurred as some sensitive issues are best broached indirectly at picnics, barbecues and banquets.

It is well documented that Chinese family life is emulated within the work setting and with it the broader societal values that ensure that social harmony and behavioral ritual are preserved (Scarborough, 1998; Yau, 1988). It is important to make this point because if business is looked at from a Western standpoint, using Western terminology, then Chinese human resource needs and expectations run the danger of being enfolded within Western meaning-frameworks. This manifests itself particularly in the "how" of human resource management activities. The overarching imperative in the West, for example, is the protestant individualistic work ethic. This is the ethical system within which management and human resource management operates. Chin (1995) describes the sociologist/philosopher Weber's thesis in which he contended that if one wanted to understand the driving force of capitalist development in Europe and North America, then one must understand the protestant work ethic.

Weber held that the protestant ethic cultivates a special type of personality that relinquishes all intermediaries between God and himself. A protestant relates from the secret inner center of his heart directly to God, which separates him from his fellow people. This relationship promotes a sense of dignity of the individual, thus bringing forth an individualism that is commensurate with the rational organization of labor (Chin, 1995:27).

In China, the ethic is often portrayed as the deep moral character of the person as s/he relates to society, of which work is either an integral part, or a sub-set. Additionally, says Fung (1948), the Chinese spirit is a synthesis of 'this world realism' and 'other world idealism', expressed as sageliness within and kingliness without. In keeping with the Tao and the natural flow of things, Chinese people chart a pragmatic path between the two.

Since the character of the sage is, according to Chinese tradition, one of sageliness within and kingliness without, the task of philosophy is to enable a man to develop this kind of character...in his inner sageliness he accomplishes spiritual cultivation; in his kingliness without he functions in society (Fung, 1948:8)

Even though there have been many management models over the years identifying management philosophy as an overarching influence on management practices (Chin, 1995; Negandhi, 1971), our research has shown little evidence of adaptation of Western management philosophy with appropriateness for the Chinese context in mind. "There is more suggestion that China has opened its doors to the West in greater measure than the West has opened its doors to China" (Whiteley, et al., 1997:77).

A major task in writing a discipline-based book such as this, especially one that advises on people management, is to make sure that somewhere, the prevailing Western orthodoxy is explained, and as importantly, challenged. It becomes even more pressing at this moment in time because the entry of China into the global business environment has produced a unique set of circumstances that could alter the shape of international management philosophy, if given the chance. A confluence of events has produced a unique situation, what the economist Brian Arthur would call "lock in" (Waldrop, 1992), that allows for a reformation of hitherto dominantly Western business ethics.

The globalization trend, the increasing need of multinationals for new and large markets, the opening of the Chinese gateway to trade, the decision by the Chinese government to educate and sophisticate its people, the size of the consumer market and the predictable change in the structure of consumer buying in China, all point to a situation where there is enough scope for the co-creation of the most productive Western and Chinese social business ethics. China has been firm in its resolve to include ideological and political development within wider economic growth (Cheng, et al., 1995). It has always been known that China, by its very size and population, is a trading force to be reckoned with, if it so wishes to be. For many years, China was open to trade in a limited sense. It showed a preference for 'hands-off' in its relations with the overseas business scene, being part of trading activities without really joining them ideologically. Now for the first time, China has decided to become more intimately involved in the international business picture, through a set of strategic choices about its place in the world.

It is clear now that China has decided to become a world trade figure (Cheng, et al., 1994). It has developed policies to upgrade literacy throughout the country and not only in major zones, regions and cities. It has recognized the usefulness of universal business practices such as English as a business language and international legal and fiscal conventions. However, we need to be careful not to confuse a willingness to join the trading sector with an acceptance of the validity of the Western ethics upon which modern business has been predicated. These include the protestant ethic and ideology-free (except for profit) capitalism. In the West, as we have seen, the focus is on individual achievement and separation of work from family life (and indeed most other areas of life). The relatively laissez faire attitudes to socially defined workplace relations are almost directly in contrast with China's stated social and relational preferences (Cheng, et al., 1995).

Whilst in China there is a pattern of fairly stable (if tacit) inclusion of a person's work as part of family life, this is not so in the West. In many Western countries, expectations vary greatly. This is partly because relatedness in business is not part of societal norms. Companies who expect people to be 'company men and women' are as valid as those who are happy with workers who have an 'I'll put in my eight hours a day and then I'm out of here' attitude. In the West, there is a widespread disassociation between home and work. It would not be uncommon in the West to tell workers not to bring their personal problems to work or to send them to professional counselors (outsourcing the problems).

It would be very unusual for a leader to be seen as any sort of buffer, especially emotional or financial. In writing about Western human resource functions in particular, well-defined, controlled and integrated structures, systems and processes produce a sense of security and certainty that appears to have become an ever more desired state. Well-delineated and impersonal structures and systems are the vehicle for communicating important relationship rituals in contrast to the suggestive and relational Chinese societal norms that overlay structures and systems in the workplace. Western human resource functions and systems aim to instill order into the intuitive, spontaneous, often irrational, side of humans at work (Champy, 1995; Weisbord, 1987). Yet the fact remains that many of these same, well established, safe, functions will soon be found inadequate to deal with anticipated turbulence in international and global business (Stacey, 1998).

The future, permeated as it will be with more ambiguity than certainty, may be more compatible with the suggestive and generative qualities of Chinese language and behaviors than the precise and definitive Western ones. Language to Chinese people is a source of fun and constant improvisation. In a meeting of several doctoral scholars (at Lingnan University) some Chinese philosophical concepts were being explained in English. Very soon people were darting up to the board, writing Chinese characters and strenuously debating possible meaning in the various forms of Chinese language. The group was focused. The atmosphere was electric, fun and stimulating. Here was the heart of the pleasure in suggestiveness. Superimposed upon the conversation was a sensitive regard for 'face', especially considering that guanxi was being cemented. These are examples of fluid and flexible and responsive ways to communicate socially. The Western need for precision in language, specificity of words, and the quest to eliminate ambiguity, would have had no place and no meaning in this communication where content and relationship-building went hand in hand.

Such methods of communicating are well established in business, say CEOs in our recent study on Chinese leadership (Wood, et al., 1999). Spontaneous, interactive, reciprocal, social dimensions of business conduct provide pragmatic ways of oiling the wheels of transactions (Chang & Holt,

1996). The best way to read the chapters on human resource functions that follow, then, is to keep asking questions about the prevailing philosophies behind them and whether they are still valid in explaining the morally as well as materially right way to do business for the people in China. "A mellow understanding of life and of human nature is, and always has been, the Chinese ideal of character and from that understanding other qualities are derived, such as pacifism, contentment, calm and strength of endurance which distinguish the Chinese character. When a man has cultivated these virtues through mental discipline, we say he has developed his character" Lin Yutang (1939). Lin was concerned that moral character of the Chinese would be adversely affected by Western principles and this is still something that needs to be taken into account when overlaying Western methodologies onto a deep yet contrasting culture.

Human Resource Management in the West

The history of the philosophical and methodological background leading to the particular conceptualization of human resource management in the West was as precise and scientific, as controlled and predictable as the best scientific minds could make it. "Philosophy as the science which by the natural light of reason studies the first causes or highest principles of all things" was the superiority of reason, fact, objectivity and measurement. (Scruton, 1997:8). Language was precise to the point that early philosophers spent entire lifetimes arguing about the precise definition of words, since words had to represent what they were seen to be (Chia, 1997). This was called representational language (Tsoukas, 1998). The precision of terms found its way into human resource and quality management systems such as the job description, job evaluation and the personnel specification. Entire performance management systems were based on the ability to precisely define goals, targets, documented processes, and to equally precisely state methods of achieving them.

In keeping with the spirit of this introduction to human resource strategy, we need to ask "What if the thinking had gone in another way?" Since the availability of supercomputers and a fundamental change in scientific thinking, such a possibility is happening right now in the very scientific areas that became a model for management systems. The notion of complex adaptive systems (Holland, 1995; Kauffman, 1991) and its philosophical import will be explored in chapter 6 of the book . Further, it will be related to some of the very natural Chinese activities such as face-working and guanxi building that are singularly suggestive and generative rather than precise and controlled (Wood et al., 1999). The reason for mentioning this development is to emphasize that, as Einstein noted, theory is the free invention of the human mind, including the theory of the workplace. Such theory, then, is not an actuality, but rather a mental creation.

What has been created can be uncreated, recreated and better still, co-recreated. The days of the scientific and control era for human resource management may be coming to an end in any case, as organizations are faced with highly differentiated product markets, short runs, internet-paced consumer changes in demand and information-age speed in transactions. People better fitted to this environment (in a human resource sense) must be flexible, able to live with a constantly changing environment, self reliant and self organizing. They should not need externally imposed policies, procedures and manuals to tell them what to do, or when and how to do it. As we see by the way human resource management has developed, the traditional framework of integrated and standardized systems has not produced enabling qualities of self-organizing and independence.

Human Resource Management (HRM) is a term coined in the West. It started off as personnel management, a function for keeping attendance, leave and sickness records as well as performing a welfare role. Lupton (1975) described the function as a repository of knowledge. The personnel model could be called basic or fundamental, one of the three typologies suggested later in the chapter.

Above all it was functional. Typically, the personnel process would begin with a department sending its required manpower figures to "personnel". A series of procedures for recruitment and selection would be triggered. Personnel would do the recruitment advertising and screening and the requesting department would do the selection, leaving the subsequent administration of the selected (and rejected) applicant(s) to personnel people. A similar system would be in place for induction. Templates were often in place so that health and safety, pay, sickness and leave arrangements and so on provided a nucleus for the induction program. Various inputs would be made from supervisors, managers and visitors. Training would typically be job or task oriented and either on the job, or conducted in training sessions. Managers would go on courses that were either technical or job specific and relevant paperwork would be completed by the personnel department.

Compensation was usually to a formula of basic and overtime rates and was administered in consultation with unions or worked out under national agreements. Payroll administration was based on attendance and timekeeping records, overtime records and data on items like sickness and annual leave. Labor turnover was calculated by the personnel department which also conducted exit interviews and sent information to appropriate departments. As you can see, these were all functional and reactive activities, performed to order and there was little evidence of either a big picture view or one that linked together the various aspects of people management. The word we have used to describe this approach is 'fundamental'.

It took some time for the range of people-oriented activities to expand. There was what could be called a transitional period. This period was not written about as such, since it was a transition that happened naturally in an evolutionary way. For example in England, large organizations began to think about the bigger picture of organizational, management and employee development. This put pressure on academics to develop theories for, and make sense of, what was happening. Over time, there developed a theoretical base for explaining and describing how to allocate and utilize people strategically and optimally (Kitay, 1997). Professional institutes such as the (then) Institute of Personnel Management, (now the Institute for People Development) in the United Kingdom, operated on a basis of what we might call practical rigor, offering professional and practical models and at the same time, requiring members to pass professional examinations that incorporated both theory and technical skill.

In the public sector, institutions such as the Institute of Manpower Studies (UK) employed a range of professionals and academics to develop and comment on personnel issues of the day. A great number of these centered around training, as the country set about developing its national youth and adult training strategies (Whiteley, 1988). The important point about this transitional period was that there was an investment by government, through an establishment called the Manpower Services

Commission (MSC) in "leading and inspiring employers, unions, training providers, national and local education services, young people, parents, the media – in truth all the specialised policies and all of the general public" (Whiteley, 1988:42) to identify problems and find specific solutions.

A wider remit began to be recognized in which various major personnel functions went through a 'problems and solutions' phase so that fledgling paradigms, assumptions, methodologies and methods for 'good' practices emerged. Gradually these led to a reconceptualization of personnel management as human resource management. There was a hope of upgrading the function to one of centrality to organizations' strategic goals (Legge, 1988). Other functions such as production, finance and marketing had already achieved this, helped by the fact that their activities were substantive and easily connected to profit through input-outputs ratios.

A first point to bear in mind, then, was that personnel management, with its fundamental and functional activities, did not suddenly metamorphose to the more sophisticated human resource management concept. Government, public and private sector organizations, professional institutes, academics and practitioners, worked sometimes independently and sometimes together to produce an ethic, and a body of knowledge to match the ethic. This in turn prescribed the parameters of human resource practices. Yet it is the Western sophisticated result that is often presented by multinationals to their partners (who are just as sophisticated within their own cultural settings and in the case of China's classical history even more so). What can non-Western organizations do except try to comprehend what is required, and where possible harmonize, what seem like competing values?

Many researches and reports assume this sophisticated methodology to be the benchmark. The danger is that what is reported is *not yet* actually practically possible. This has been one of the major findings in our research. One can argue that it will only be a matter of time before practices catch up with the sophisticated design and reporting system, and that there is a readymade sophistication available for China as it enters the human resource management sector. However what input China has had in order to evolve to its own brand of sophistication is not clear at this point. This leads to another problem.

The problem is that the sophisticated human resource edifice is based on the Western cultural foundation, reflecting the protestant (individualistic) work ethic as it was translated into very practical and functional action. Scientific management expressed Western scientific philosophy as it related to the management of people. (Weisbord, 1987). There was a prescribed reality presented to managers in the way of operational tasks and targets. These were described precisely, accurately and objectively (people being one of the objective factors of production). Helped by such scientific methodologies as time and motion studies (Gilbreth, 1911) the achievement of tasks and targets was translated into efficient use of human movements. Humans were part of a machine-like calculative psychological contract (Etzioni, 1971).

As time went on, it was discovered that people had an emotional side and that this side was an influential factor in productivity. The theory developed, largely in the USA, (Roethlisberger & Dixon, 1939) that people at work had social and emotional needs and that if these needs were met, workers would become more productive. A more benign and human prescribed reality replaced the machine-like first version (Herzberg, 1966; Maslow, 1970). Managers were encouraged to examine their assumptions about what workers brought to the workplace (McGregor, 1960). The prescribed nature of work was somewhat overtaken, theoretically anyway, by the very unprescriptive notion of participative management (Emery, 1993) and the learning organization (Senge, 1992).

One of the outcomes of this development was that people were no longer perceived as robot-like extensions of machines. Another was that the individual nature of the person as a thoughtful and decisive being became even more heavily emphasized. Instead of managers prescribing a set reality to workers, the idea of managers negotiating reality together with workers became installed in such vehicles as the quality movement (Nadler, 1998) and industrial relations (see Figure 1). One of the latest examples of this is the notion of individual workplace agreements (Whiteley, 1999a) where the worker is, theoretically, free to enter directly into a bargain with the employer.

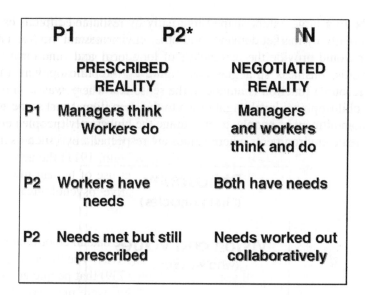

P1	P2*	N
	PRESCRIBED REALITY	**NEGOTIATED REALITY**
P1	**Managers think Workers do**	**Managers and workers think and do**
P2	**Workers have needs**	**Both have needs**
P2	**Needs met but still prescribed**	**Needs worked out collaboratively**

Figure 1. From prescribed to negotiated reality

Another element of sophistication has been the integration across functional departments and the establishment, where possible, of interdepartmental interdependencies. It seems from the more recent management writers (especially those anticipating the changes required to meet turbulent times ahead) that even though there may be an overlay of behavioral aspects such as worker participation in work design and decision making, *the structural functionalist foundation of scientific management has been preserved* (Briggs, 1989; Morgan, 1997; Zohar, 1994). Structural functionalism presents a contrast to the Chinese preference for a more holistic and relational structure, to be integrated with Chinese family values as an integral part of organizational design.

Keeping this in mind, we can look at the points of entry for human resource management assuming it has achieved a central position. To fulfil its role of enabling the organization to achieve its mission and business strategies, human resource management must be part of a hierarchical flow of activities. The business ideology, from this perspective, would come first, and from this the corporate vision and values would emerge as cultural benchmarks. The business mission, i.e. the organization's purpose and scope, would be to a large extent shaped internally by skills and capital resources and externally by market demands and other environmental factors. The two together would provide the parameters of long term goals and priorities, in other words, business strategies (see figure 2). We can see here that the human resource function is unique in the sense that it is pervasive. From the highest philosophical levels right down to the shop floor, there is the need to obtain commitment of people, to encourage the highest performance possible and to create environments where values are respected and standards met.

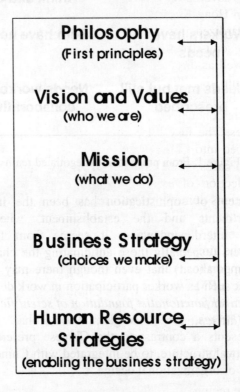

Figure 2. Human Resource Management as part of the business strategy

Human Resource Management Strategies and Practices in Foreign Invested Enterprises in the PRC: The 1997 study

Following the 1996 study described in chapter 1, which gathered data from 156 organizations, our research team met in 1997 to design an interview schedule that would reflect the 1996 findings whilst allowing for any emerging issues. This was an in depth study, qualitative and case oriented. It was planned to develop a semi-structured interview using a team of interviewers from Hong Kong and China. To achieve as high reliability as possible, a standardized introduction was collaboratively designed. Again collaboratively, a semi-structured interview schedule was designed to allow conversation as well as directed responses to questions. The interview sites were mostly within the PRC, and Hong Kong with the proviso that all organizations did business in China. The interviews were either recorded and transcribed or were conducted by at least two people, one of whom was able to take field notes. The PRC cases were conducted in both Mandarin and English, transcribed into Chinese and then into English. Some of the Hong Kong and other cases were conducted in English. In addition to the interviews, a selection of existing Hong Kong case examples of multi national organizations demonstrating strategic human resource management were used.

Specifically, the aims of the phase two interviews were to:
- clarify and support (or otherwise) the 1996 findings;
- investigate the HRM strategies and practices in FIEs in PRC in more depth and with some reasons/explanations/examples;
- identify any difficulties and concerns encountered by FIEs in the PRC;
- identify how the Western model was perceived to fit into the Chinese culture;
- investigate the reciprocity of both cultures in terms of human resource arrangements.

Taking the lead from the 1996 findings, questions were asked about business strategy formulation, implementation and communication. These were followed by questions relating to human resource strategies and practices. In the next chapter we discuss the role and practice of human resource management strategies, however in this chapter we focus on a discussion of the role of business strategy in the PRC and Hong Kong.

Business strategy theory and concepts

> *Top level managers in many of today's leading corporations are losing control of their companies. The problem is not that they have misjudged the demands created by an increasingly complex environment and an accelerating twenty years, strategic thinking has far outdistanced organizational capabilities rate of environmental change, nor even that they failed to develop strategies appropriate to the new challenges. The problem is that their organizations are incapable of carrying out the sophisticated strategies they have developed (Bartlett, and Ghoshal, 1996).*

The quotation above is particularly important when investigating multi- or single national corporations well developed enough to invest in China under either joint venture or more recently sole trading arrangements. Business strategy is presented here as a context for human resource strategy. The assumption is that the chosen strategic approach circumscribes appropriate human resource strategies.

The conventional wisdom of the strategy planning schools (Ansoff, 1990; Ansoff, 1991; Porter, 1980; Porter, 1985) involves analyzing relationships between products and markets and working out the key features of the organization as they fit the market in terms of offering opportunities for competitiveness and growth. Typically, internal planning takes the form of analyzing the value chain in terms of logistics, operations, marketing and services (primary activities), procurement and technology development (support activities), human resource management and other management systems (support activities).

A strong characteristic of the planning school is the assumption that managers work from carefully planned rational actions. Mintzberg (1988) exploded this myth (and produced some others) when he studied what senior managers actually did. Instead of the manager being a reflective systematic planner, s/he worked at a relentless pace, where time was very often hijacked by subordinates and where the work was fragmented, brief, and varied.

Mintzberg helps to compare strategy approaches by presenting three contrasting modes - the entrepreneurial mode, the adaptive mode and the planning mode (table 1).

Characteristic	Entrepreneurial	Adaptive	Planning
Motives for decisions	Proactive	Reactive	Pro and reactive
Goals of organization	Growth	Indeterminate	Efficiency, growth
Evaluation proposals	Judgmental	Judgmental	Analytical
Choices made by	Entrepreneur	Bargaining	Management
Decision horizon	Long term	Short Term	Long Term
Decision linkages	Loosely coupled	Disjointed	Integrated
Flexibility	Flexible	Flexible	Constrained
Objectives of org	Operational	Non-operational	Operational
Org. Environment	Yielding	Complex/Dynamic	Predictable/stable
Source of power	Entrepreneur	Divided	Management

Table 1. Four modes of Strategic Planning

Adapted from Mintzberg, H. (1988). "Strategy Making in Three Modes." In J. Quinn, H. Mintberg and R. James. *The Strategy Process: Concepts, Contexts and Cases*. Englewood Cliffs, N.J., Prentice Hall International, page 87.

Each of these modes mean different requirements of the human resource manager in terms of appropriate management styles, necessary structures and systems of reward and communication. Contrasting the entrepreneurial and planning modes, it is easy to observe that very different types of human resource support systems would be needed for each.

In addition to the strategic planning mode, the human resource strategist needs to dovetail human resource strategies with the organization's preference for dealing with the environment. Here Miles and Snow's (1980) typologies *of defenders, prospectors, analyzers, and reactors* is useful. There is the need to use human resource strategies to activate the chosen business strategies (often in the face of new and changing strategies). This responsiveness to the various levels of organizational design and development is a key responsibility of human resource management. Preparing people for a future that could be very different, reinforcing a culture so that values are harmonious with the organization/environment and being able to provide flexibility so that people can respond to a change in strategic choice helps organizational competitiveness.

Another layer of discussion is needed when applying strategic formulation and implementation in foreign settings. This is best captured by the *etic/emic* categorization (Brislin, 1976). The etic concept refers to aspects of culture such as language, rituals, mores and other social frameworks that may be somewhat universalistic in nature. The implication is that humans, in their organization of social settings, are similar in some ways. Etic suggests a sense of generalizability and confidence that something, a topic, ethic or activity will be understood across national and cultural boundaries. For example, there is an etic flavor to the way societies develop key organizing principles. Almost all organized groups have authority and power structures (like Hofstede's notion of power distance) (Hofstede, 1980) and these are often realized through family and other social devices. Relationships to time (Trompenaars, 1998) seem to be important in all societies.

Societies usually have moral rules of some sort in operation. They have educational methodologies for making sure that these are taught and reinforced (Bond, 1989) and moral or legalistic laws for making sure that they are obeyed. The general existence of power and authority, time, education, socializing and sanctioning are obvious in the range of primitive to sophisticated societies. However, the way that these principles are translated into norms, rules and regulations could not be more different in most cases. Each society imprints its own 'cultural signature' on the way these principles are enacted. These relate the way each society philosophizes the 'right' way and the 'good' way to live. These very unique, locally situated interpretations and prescriptions are expressed as emic. Emic is best described as particularistic and local in nature, subject to the nuances and codified social rules that make it comfortable to obey, and uncomfortable to disregard (figure 3).

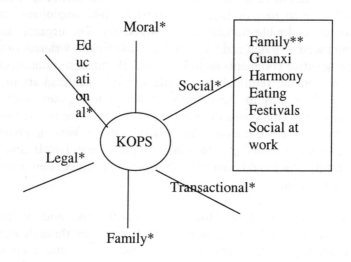

Figure 3. Key Organizing Principles (KOPS), Etic and Emic

In our conversations with both Chinese and Western leaders, we were left with the impression that whilst the concept of business strategy formulation itself seemed to be an etic, the activities surrounding it (including questions about who decides on the strategy and how it is communicated) were very much emic in nature. A similar comment could be made about human resource strategy. Whilst it may be reasonably safe to describe the existence of named human resource activities (e.g., recruitment and selection, training, performance appraisal, compensation), there are likely to be Chinese social and cultural principles making these activities uniquely different in practice. In other words the name does not imply the behavior. An example of the 'performance appraisal process' from one of our case organizations shows the unnecessary personal conflict that can arise if this is not understood.

Following Western best practice, a performance system was installed where the 'rater-to ratee' interview was conducted face to face (or, implied, "loss of face to loss of face"). As well as this, employees completed a questionnaire, double translated into Mandarin. The organization's senior managers were irritated and frustrated because first, it was almost impossible to elicit negative comments on individual performance and secondly because the scores on the returned questionnaire rarely deviated from the central tendency. This was to the extreme. When a four point scale was used, supervisors and employees invented a spot between the points two and three so that they could score around (an invisible) mean. We conversed indirectly (over dim sum) about this to some of the Chinese staff and managers. Interestingly, they said that most people understood the need for some performance control.

There was therefore little problem with the etic of performance monitoring. This did happen in practice. It was done through a combination of 'uncles and aunties' who criticized, encouraged and even unofficially trained people when necessary. This operated together with an approach called "the iron hand in the velvet glove". Good performance meant good face and it was up to everybody to bring on those who needed it "or to chase away those who were not pulling their weight". To attempt to describe the informal process in Western terms would prove difficult, because much of the explanation involved tacit knowledge (Schein, 1993). That is, knowledge built upon cultural understanding of how things should work to preserve important Chinese social values.

The lesson to be learned from such stories is that a functional name may be accepted as part of business language, such as human resource functional names. However it is not useful to go much beyond the use of generic terms to describe functions. As soon as they are activated, a layer of meaning needs to be overlaid in keeping with the values of the home culture. It is in this spirit that we relay the findings on our questions about the typical business strategies used by Foreign Invested Enterprises in China.

Certain business strategies have long been accepted in the West as competitive strategic choices. Schuler and Jackson (1987) produced a model that linked business strategies to what he called "effective human resource strategies or human resource philosophies" (Tyson, 1995:107). Cost reduction strategies were linked to hard and specific human resource policies and practices and quality standards could be included in these. Organizations choosing innovation applied softer human resource approaches, more in keeping with the need for intrinsic motivation to keep producing intellectual capital than the extrinsic (often short term) motivation of the contract. The facilitative, or ad hoc and flexible approach meant organizations could respond as needed within the other two (see figure 4).

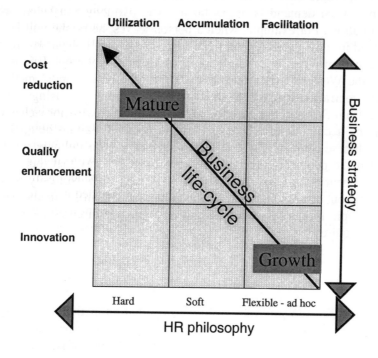

Figure 4. Business Strategy and Differentiated Human Resource approaches

Adapted from Tyson, S (1995). *Human Resource Strategy: Towards a general theory of Human Resource Management*. London: Pitman, page 107.

However, this argument follows the Western ideas upon which the model was built. Part of this thinking is the way that relationships are often presented as linear and directional. When applying some of the inbuilt relational values to the matching of business strategy with human resource approaches in China, things need to be handled differently.

The human resource manager in China will already be aware of the adaptations necessary to translate such Western models as Schuler and Jackson's (1987) utilizer, accumulator and facilitator into acceptable practice. For example, within the Chinese system, there would be a more holistic and continuous, even circular alternative to the linear, strategy based relationship. It would only be possible to utilize someone, even on a short contract and casual demand basis, as far as face, harmony and behavioral ritual would allow. For example, when a person leaves, he or she will have been inducted into the guanxi system, have become part of colleagues' lives and will be part of a reciprocal network of obligations in future. This is in contrast to the Western 'when the job ends the relationship ends' method (known as contractualism). The model below (figure 5), using some dimensions from Scarborough (1998), suggests how the two approaches of utilization and accumulation, (hard and soft respectively) could be applied within the Chinese contexts. The overlay would cater for the cultural 'musts' that would make people comfortable at work Note the way that the circle replaces the linear vector and that there is no end as such. Not only is the model circular but dimensions such as guo quing, face, guanxi, yin and yang are kaleidoscopic in nature, reshaping and reforming as circumstances and pragmatism requires.

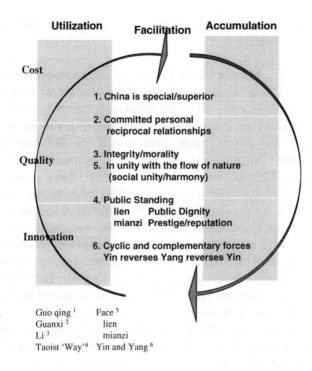

Figure 5. Business strategies, human resource approaches and social values

Obeying cultural mores and applying the cultural overlay to the management of people will be second nature to Chinese managers. It is when the use of Western-style formal human resource functions is introduced that problems arise. Yet, like the use of Business English, these are required for etic purposes. Performance appraisal as a term has international uses. Difficulties arise when managers rely on the content and conventions as well as the framework of Western human resource management for guidance on how to recruit, train, motivate and reward people. Theory, in books and in other academic and professional literature tends, over time, to describe what comes to be taken as 'received wisdom'. Currently the formalized assumptions and concepts appear more Western than Chinese. This danger was indicated in our research and there was a discernable sense that some of the more sophisticated human resource activities were given lip service but were not actually practised.

It is necessary but not sufficient in the literature on human resource management in China to devote the requisite chapter or section on cross cultural theory before going on to use Western terminology (job evaluation, manpower planning, merit systems, empowerment, quality of working life). In some cases the use is made with sensitivity and cultural empathy (Torrington, 1994). Nevertheless, the very terms themselves are conceptually foreign to some Chinese values. It is clear that China is a country with intuitive and consistent entrepreneurial ability, the excuse that therefore Western methods are necessary to improve business skill and acumen is not plausible. Some natural activities in the Chinese setting would be prized in the West such as 'family', guanxi and face working, and yet, these tend to be expressed as Western constructs of team work, networking and interpersonal skills. Up to the point of carrying out and reporting our research in this book, we too were using Western functional language. What we are suggesting is the adoption of some of the already well established Chinese terms in figure 3 as human resource terminology. As this has not yet been done, we will report our findings in the way that they were researched but we are aware that change in human resource terminology needs to happen.

Business Strategy Findings

Three dominant business strategies, quality, cost reduction and innovation were reported from the 1996 study It was found in both the 1996 (Tang, et al., 1996) and 1997 (Whiteley, et al., 1997) studies that organizations used combined business strategies (table 2).

Types	Frequency	Percent
Quality + cost reduction	35	36.5
Quality + innovation	22	22.9
Quality, cost reduction + innovation	39	40.6

Table 2. Typologies of Business Strategies

We were interested to find out how organizations managed to harmonize what looked to us like competing strategies. Noting Tyson's (1995:7) point (that classifying strategic direction risks oversimplification, and that several apparently contradictory strategies might be in place at any one time with movement from innovation through cost control and quality), we still felt that there was some sense in Porter's (1985) generic strategies idea. We therefore followed the multiple strategies indication in the 1996 study through to the 1997 study. The strategies used were confirmed as popular ones and interestingly, foreign invested enterprises were comfortable with the multiple strategy approach dominated by quality. The quality strategy appeared to be more of a corporate strategy, applied across the portfolios of invested businesses, than a particular market based choice.

We pressed the point that cost control and rationalization could compete with achieving consistently high quality which, in turn, could compete with innovation as a business strategy, requiring as it would rapid and flexible market entry and exits, and creative thinking to continually differentiate products and services. There was surprising uniformity in the answers. Quality was not negotiable. Costs minimization was necessary and where possible, particularly with technology, innovation would be fostered.

Hong Kong enterprises operating in Hong Kong

We have drawn briefly on cases we researched in Hong Kong because the idea is to take some organizations that are well established and yet have faced some of the challenges currently facing FIEs in China. In this way, some contrasts and comparisons can be made. Three areas, business strategy, human resource strategy and human resource practices have been selected for this purpose. Hong Kong enterprises operating in Hong Kong (HK/HK) included a prominent bank, a large social club, a hospital organization, a food service organization, an office supplies business, insurance, a holdings group, a container terminal and an airline.

All enterprises in the HK/HK data set had clearly stated long term goals. In most cases these goals appeared to have matured over time. Dominant strategies espoused by most enterprises were *Quality* "to provide quality merchandise at good value", "The highest level of service to customers", *Professionalism*, *Innovation* "to pursue innovation to keep ahead of the competition", and *Profit* as "good financial performance".

The following set of long-term objectives was a fair indication of the way Hong Kong business strategy statements were expressed.

- Achieve an acceptable return on investments, produce superior financial returns
- Maintain a significant market share
- Provide high quality service: be totally customer driven
- Be a good employer, provide quality working conditions, maximize individual potential, treasure staff as valuable assets

Some Hong Kong operations counted being a good employer and corporate citizen as a business strategy "to provide rewarding and enjoyable careers for staff, to accept responsibility towards the environment, to be committed to the communities [we] serve and to the future of Hong Kong". Quality and Innovation strategies such as those suggested in the FIEs in the PRC were prominent also in the Hong Kong enterprises but cost was not specifically indicated, rather it was expressed as profitability and good financial performance. Surprisingly, given Schuler and Jackson's (1987) model, as the organization matured, the attitude to cost (control to optimization) increased. The finding in the 1996 study, that the quality enhancement business strategy was most supported and that this was strongly linked to customer service was upheld in the case interviews.

Hong Kong enterprises operating in the PRC

It was clear by the responses that the business strategies reflected the parent company's philosophy of the business. Strategically the PRC was preferred because of relatively cheap land and labor (although for specialized hi-tech organizations "young talent" was considered to be difficult to obtain and retain). There was constant reference to the predicted large size, or "significant market potential" of the PRC market as an inducement to invest in the China. Suggested constraints on business strategies included not too much spending power, although this was changing especially in the big cities. Emphasized throughout the interviews was the recurring constraint of low skill levels, poor work attitudes, poor loyalty to the employer and a reluctance to take responsibility and accountability. These constraints were referred to in our "outlook from China".

As mentioned before, there were no cases of a single business strategy. Quality enhancement seemed to be overarching and this was expressed variously as product quality, service quality and the quality of human resources. Other business strategies were expansion and business development. The cost reduction business strategy was reframed by the respondents who preferred to consider notions of cost efficiency and added-value.

PRC-based Foreign Invested Enterprises

Four aspects of business strategy were of particular interest in understanding the current business strategy situation of the PRC-based enterprises: What is the dominant strategy; who decides the strategy; how is it communicated and what are the long and short term goals?

What is the dominant strategy?

The 1996 and 1997 findings were similar although further exploration on the "no one single strategy" theme suggested that some of the business strategies may not have been mainstream but developmental or remedial. These strategies had to provide a focus as there was some concern about PRC capabilities in comparison with FIE parent organizations, both in the quality and cost structures areas.

Concerning the unanimous concern with *Quality* as a business strategy, every respondent either named it as the dominant strategy or pointed out that the enterprise was already a world leader in quality and it wanted to remain that way. It was evident that the strategy was to bring the PRC operation up to the International Standards Organization (ISO) or other recognized quality standards installed by the parent. The types of quality described were quality of product, quality of service and after sales service. Over half of the organizations interviewed specifically mentioned ISO awards and/or other prestigious quality awards and all were working towards installing or improving quality control/quality improvement systems in the PRC.

The next well subscribed strategy was the advancement or transfer of *technology* (see table 3). For those FIEs who already had leading technology there was a strategy of technology transfer. This included technology innovation and many of the respondents saw this as a competitive advantage. For those who did not want to adopt the transfer strategy, arrangements were being made for PRC-based research and development, sometimes on a large scale. The preference seemed to be to foster technology development rather than effect a straight transfer, especially for those organizations who were planning on being in China for the long term, and figures of fifty years were not uncommon. In contrast, those organizations who were basing their business strategy on the attraction of cheap labor, yet whose product relied on technology, either sent their own technical people or used their 'last version' technology for production in China. These companies also included the cost reduction of labor as a condition for business competitiveness.

Dominant Strategy	Number of companies
Quality / product; service; after sales service	14
Technology / transfer [t]; PRC-based R&D [d]	[t] 5, [d] 2, [t+d] 2.
Innovation*	
Cost / control [c]; reduction [r] ;value [v]	[c] 5, [r] 2, [v] 1.
Labor Force advantage	5
Others (sales; innovation;	5
Combination	19

Table 3. Business Strategy

*Innovation was referred to alongside technology

Cost reduction was the next most popular business strategy. This was interpreted in different ways. Keeping production costs down was seen as an ancillary strategy for many companies, except where there was so much confidence in the quality of, and demand for, the product that cost was not needed as a strategy. Examples of this were a pharmaceuticals company, a tyre manufacturing company, one in consumer durables and two food producing/distribution organizations. However almost all organizations were interested in effective control of costs and a value-adding costing procedures.

Innovation was not as strongly reflected as the other strategies but it was mentioned several times in connection with technology. Using Schuler and Jackson's (1987) model for linking business strategies to human resource strategies an interesting scenario developed. In many ways it illustrates the problem of organizations who choose business strategies that require multiple and not always compatible human resource strategies.

Our business strategy data suggested that it was commonplace for more than one business strategy to be in operation. The cost reduction strategy would match well with the utilizer human resource strategy. Human resources would be deployed efficiently, often by cutting costs through short-term employment as well as task skilling. The quality strategy would match with the accumulator human resource strategy. Here, almost the opposite approach is taken. There would be an investment in people, recruitment and development of people with potential so as to accumulate a wealth of knowledge and skills. Harmonizing these in the business processes sense might be easier than in the human resource sense, especially in this formative period of Chinese development. It is difficult to encourage people to be flexible and at the same time to be compliant and precise, to reach for high quality whist cutting costs, even within a sophisticated context.

Who decides business strategy?

In around half of the companies interviewed the parent organization set the business strategy (Table 4). In four of the cases, only the parent set the strategy. In the others, the parent and the Chinese and Foreign general managers set the strategy together and often the Board of Directors would endorse the strategies. In a couple of the cases, the foreign partner did not become involved in the business at all, restricting the involvement to the setting of targets for taking profits out of the company. Here the Chinese general manager set the strategy within defined profit parameters.

Parent company	10
Board of Directors	8
General Managers \ foreign	5
General Managers \ PRC	8
Senior Management (foreign or PRC)	1
Combination	11

Table 4. Who decides Strategy?

How were strategies communicated?

The pattern was that the parent developed the strategy, often with general managers, communicated it to general managers if necessary, who then communicated it to the department heads. Ten of the PRC based organizations did not see the need to communicate the business strategy to the general workforce. Those that did were also the organizations that held a long term and developmental view of the workforce and used either a transitional or sophisticated Human Resource model. All companies used the departmental head as a lynch-pin to communicate the business strategy to the workforce, or, in some cases, sub-contractors.

Parent to/with GMs (foreign/PRC)	10
Board of Directors to GMs	6
General Managers to Dept Heads	16
Any of the above to all employees	10
Combination	13

Table 5. How is Strategy Communicated?

An immediate and important contrast between both the Hong Kong in Hong Kong (HK in HK) cases, Hong Kong in the PRC and the PRC-based cases was the need each of these groups felt to communicate the business strategy to the employees. HK in HK organizations all, without exception, brought employees into the picture. Strategies to encourage commitment were creative and comprehensive. Hong Kong companies operating in the PRC were also conscious of the employee's role in making profit. They saw the need to involve them in knowing about strategies but used simpler methods of communication. PRC-based organizations were not so willing to include employees into the strategic communications network.

PRC-based respondents said that employees had difficulties understanding the notion of strategy and also the notion of why they needed to understand it. However some, notably those who had a long-term view and followed the sophisticated model (integrating HR with the business strategy and having an integrated HR strategy), had comprehensive communication strategies even though they knew that they would not be readily understood as yet.

Concerning communication in general (including the communicating of strategy), there was a wide range of methods used, as described below. This is consistent with a transitional strategy. The use of communication devices varied. In some cases communication was used simply to pass on orders. In others it was seen as a tool to help implement corporate strategy. There was a contrast between the number of Hong Kong-based and PRC-based enterprises in this regard. In the Hong Kong cases, communication was almost always linked to corporate culture and values. In the PRC this was almost the opposite, giving the sense of 'need to know' rather than 'share important information' and this was most noticeable at the general worker level. Communication-wise, it would seem that some enterprises were still operating a fundamental, internally-focused model.

Examples of communication responses:

General manager meets with dept heads to set business goals/quarterly meeting informs employees of quarterly goals and directions/video showing previous quarter's overall performance is shown/notice boards and displays are used by promotions to reinforce the message/employees are encouraged to share ideas and some of these are put into writing and are presented to the general manager; From [Parent] to gen manager PRC/gen manager PRC to dept heads who have monthly meetings to explain the plan/ Communist party meetings (operations) serve as a bridge between upper and lower levels. Dept heads often hold dinner parties/vertical communication at annual dinner parties;

General staff do not necessarily need to know strategy details/when there is a major issue such as housing problem, representatives from the staff union will have direct dialogues with managers. This happens once or twice a year/Communications between top management and department heads are carried out through management meetings. Such meetings are held very frequently and are attended by the General Manager, top level managers, and department heads directly reporting to them;

We have annual leadership meetings/use large display board to communicate goals and policy/company newsletter/weekly administration. We have meeting/dept heads meetings, station chiefs and section leader morning briefings. We have 2-monthly meetings so that staff can bring up their thoughts and ideas to be answered by general manager/ departments can communicate with each other.

We have a downward flow from General manager to heads to supervisors to workers; All recruits are informed of the company policy;

Dept heads meet to digest the strategy and twice daily production meetings are held. Workers sign an 'internal contract or "agreement documents" signifying their commitment to the company. Everyone is aware of who the manager is and there are daily and often informal reports;

The General Manager's Company plan and policy are discussed at the weekly Departmental Head Meeting. The General Manager also uses questionnaires and interviews to collect staff opinions. Before production, units will have an overview of the production plan and manpower allocation The managers of these production units will make use of this monthly meeting or meals to communicate;

This last example shows the way that the more formal and rational communication design is integrated with the networking and groupness, including the General Manager, into the communication process.

The flow of information is an important tool when it comes to putting corporate strategy into effect. Staff are encouraged to share information and experiences and to strengthen vertical and internal exchanges. Information is formally sent through the following channels; key information concerning business operation is regularly given to the general staff. Information concerning various department is passed to their respective departmental heads. Inter-departmental communication is achieved mainly by the exchange of information about business operations. A special department has been set up to educate the employees about corporate culture and company strategy. This department is in charge of producing the Company's newsletter; "Striving For Continuous Improvement". The newsletter helps to increase unity and co-operation between departments and to improve the overall the performance of the staff. To be honest and trust one another/ Openness and honesty are encouraged and much effort is put into exterminating anything which harms effective communication. It is in this way that an honest working environment is created. A Realisation Suggestion Committee has been set up. Members of this committee include the General Manager, the president of the Labour Union, the assistant manager and representatives form the Human Resources Department. The committee regularly calls 'workers' forums' in order to discuss company policies, working conditions, personal development and welfare matters and to find solutions to any problems which may exist. The minutes of the forums are published.

Long and short term goals

Of those that had long term goals (for some, immediate survival seemed to take their place) two connected and dominant goals were *to achieve or retain the position of market leader*, in the PRC and in three cases Asia. Connected to this was the long term goal of increasing market share (Table 6). In four cases, cost control was a goal followed by goals such as more effective production, localization and diversification. There was a marked absence of Human Resource goals being expressed within the   long term business setting, especially compared to the Hong Kong-based companies where this was the rule rather than the exception.   Short term goals were to focus on production, sales, customer related goals and raising profits.

Long term goals	Short term goals*
Capture more market share	Focus on Production
Become Leaders/provide best	Focus on Profits
Better/more production	Focus on Sales
Reduce Costs/Labour	Focus on Growth
Localisation **	Become better than
	Competitors
Diversify	Customer satisfaction
	Lower Price

Table 6. Long and Short term goals

*   Not all enterprises stated short term goals

** For many of the enterprises, Localisation was mentioned as an intention, if not a goal

Similarities with the Hong Kong cases were noted with the prominence of quality and expansion of market share. Differences were found mainly in the way that cost was expressed. In China this was in cost control and cost reduction whereas in Hong Kong cost was associated with value and\or cost effectiveness. In the PRC, in some cases it seemed evident that labor was perceived as a cost and that the way costs were being reduced was by saving on investment in human resource development. This applied more to the unskilled workforce, especially in areas where supply was abundant. Comparatively speaking, technology was given more prominence in the PRC interviews than in Hong Kong. However, a reason seemed to be that the technology was not at the required standard for the quality of product required. It was interesting that there seemed to be a confidence in the ability of PRC workers and managers to learn quickly and as most of the training was in the technical field, those making decisions between technology transfer and technology development may become swayed towards the latter.

4.   Human Resource Strategies in the Chinese Context

Human Resource Strategies in the Chinese context

Business organizations face challenges in achieving and maintaining a competitive edge in a rapidly changing world. These include managing growth and change in a global marketplace, introducing new technology, achieving and maintaining low costs, improving service/product quality, and balancing diversity and synergy. Addressing these business challenges requires the talents, energies, and performance of employees. How effectively business strategies are implemented depends in a large part on the management of human resources (Walker, 1992:8)

In this chapter we discuss the role of human resource strategy, as well as the theory and models which relate to actual practices of human resource strategy within PRC and Hong Kong based organizations. Learning concepts central to human resource strategy are presented in Figure 1.

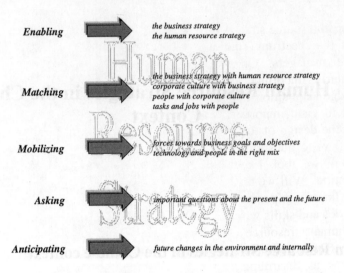

Enabling → the business strategy
the human resource strategy

Matching → the business strategy with human resource strategy
corporate culture with business strategy
people with corporate culture
tasks and jobs with people

Mobilizing → forces towards business goals and objectives
technology and people in the right mix

Asking → important questions about the present and the future

Anticipating → future changes in the environment and internally

Figure 1. Human Resource Strategy Concepts

The job of human resource strategy is to enable that part of the business strategy involving decisions about which resources to use (automate or populate). In particular, its role is to mobilize, motivate and reward workforce members in the pursuit of the organization's mission and strategic goals. Business strategies are about choices and human resource strategy is no different, being part of the process for asking questions such as those in figure 2.

Where do we need to go for a healthy future?

How do we get there in terms of human resources?

What is it that we value so much that it must be part of that future?

What do we need to dissipate and renew in order to remain strong and competitive?

Which of our human processes and behaviors can we make excellent, unique and inimitable

thereby making it difficult for others to substitute or copy?

Figure 2. Questions arising from the human resource strategy

Human resource strategy formulation needs to operate from two opposite ends of the spectrum, sometimes making things very difficult for human resource managers. On one end, strategy formulation is imaginative (particularly important as the rate and importance of technology and knowledge acquisition increases). Answers to questions about an imagined future will yield important ideas on training and reward, and bigger ideas such as the design of the organizational profile. Strategists need to imagine the answers to questions such as: Where will we be in three years time? What will we look like? Will we have offices or will we be a virtual organization? Will we take advantage of increasing consumer independence through Internet exposure by customizing instead of aggregating? What new capabilities and skills will we need to activate these decisions? The image is of a human resource strategist who is imaginative, opportunistic, entrepreneurial, and creative, able to bring together diverse energies at the same time as disarming harmful forces, and willing to tolerate risk as opportunities are grasped.

On the other end of the spectrum, the human resource manager needs to be systematic, representing a directional and stabilizing force in the organization. Questions to be asked in the here and now will be very different. Are we in alignment with business strategy or are we suffering from drift? Do our current structures reflect the way people prefer to be motivated and rewarded? Are our systems too static and in danger of being over refined? Alternatively, are they too loose and indefinite so that people become indulgent and lose the focus of the mission and business strategy as their guiding star? In the here and now, certain systems need to be constantly checked for strategic fit. In particular the communication and information systems in the organization need to fit its 'conversational style'. Choosing communication and conversational styles is not merely a technical concern (Daft, 1987). For example, if a period of radical change is foreseen, it may be wise to increase face-to-face, discussive-type communication and to de-emphasize the terse 'shorthand' styles that might serve well in times of stability and familiarity.

So the human resource planner and strategist needs to have both feet planted firmly in the present but also be looking tentatively into the future. If all that human resource management entailed was the administration of systems such as recruitment and selection, induction and training, performance appraisal, and compensation as they presently existed then the function would be better named personnel management. The twin responsibilities of combining today's order with tomorrow's uncertainties more reflect the human resource strategy concept.

Central to the notion of human resource strategy is corporate culture. Culture is, to Schein,

A pattern of shared assumptions/invented discovered and shared by a given group, as it learns to cope with its problems of external adaptation and internal integration, that has worked well enough to be valid, and therefore, is to be taught to new members of the group as the correct way to perceive, think and feel in relation to those problems (Schein, 1985:52)

The people being managed in an organization are not blank slates. Each person (within the Chinese setting this means the individual within the group) brings to work the deep and tacit 'culture rules' of society. What people value, whether this is independence or dependence, fairness or protocol, confrontation or harmony is the basis upon which their feeling of comfort rests. In the West, many people believe in fair play, promotion on merit, equality of contribution from colleagues and management alike, and the payment of rewards when they are earned (i.e. no figureheads). These beliefs become 'value rules'. They are best observed when they are infringed upon and in the West, where there are few *mianxi* and *lien* concerns, people can and do surface infringements easily, vocally and sometimes publicly. Of course, one of the problems for the Westerner in the Chinese setting is that such candor can undermine face relations so that it is of little or no use to ask for an outright answer to an instinctive feeling that cultural norms are being disturbed. One of the central norms prevents casual, face to face 'brutally honest' exchanges.

Carefully observed (or intuited) customs and practices provide evidence of Chinese cultural norms, rules and mores as they are translated into everyday life. Regular lunches with old colleagues, deprecation when singled out for individual praise, the appreciation of the reassuring touch, respectful attitudes to boss/teacher - these can be observed as patterns that cross all types of organization. As well as the things that make people comfortable, there are those in every culture that "just aren't done". Any newcomer into a culture (such as an FIE manager) usually finds out the hard (and not always direct) way about conventions that have been inadvertently contravened. Organizational culture is a sort of stretched-out personality. It is a pattern or template for forming the basis of shared understanding that helps people to know how things are done, and how they are supposed to behave.

The culture of an organization, like that of a society, is a homemade blueprint for 'seeing' the world in a particular way. Societies will organize their key elements, human relationships, resources, and social institutions to ensure survival and success (in the unique way that they themselves define them). People decide what they value greatly and they build their beliefs, attitudes, and ultimately behaviors, accordingly (Adler, 1991). The blueprint takes the form of behavior rules that have become solid enough to form everyday, well-accepted patterns of behavior that everyone knows even if they don't say so. These patterns and rules will be handed down as organizational memory or folklore. In the case of organizations, the values and beliefs will provide the 'spectacles' through which members will interpret organizational life. The patterns and rules develop into 'agreed solutions' to ways of handling threats and opportunities from the inside and outside environment.

The ideal situation in an organization is that members agree and share one code of behavior. This is not easy for multi nationals when the higher level activities such as business strategy formation are considered as an etic. The emic, uniquely local way of doing things is often implicitly accepted in the operational areas. This leads to a notion of the alignment of human resource strategy with its shop floor activities.

One of the biggest challenges in managing organizational culture where there are competing value systems lies in the fact that the codes of culture-making are symbolic. They are expressed through ritual, myth, and organizational stories and are inevitably relational in nature. Telling the organizational story, and therefore reinforcing its lore through stories, (tall but somehow always believable) are part of workers' everyday dialogue. Interestingly, we have heard many stories and anecdotes from FIE managers that reveal a growing sensitivity to Chinese cultural ways and needs. These represent the tacit side of the organization (Schein, 1993) at its least visible and yet most consequential. It is especially so when human resource managers have the job of harmonizing diverse cultures within the organization or group of companies (figure 3).

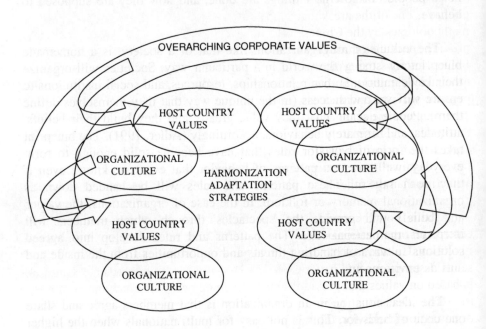

Figure 3. From corporate to organizational culture

Managing corporate culture is part of the human resource strategist's remit, particularly if there is impending change of such a nature that performance indicators themselves need to change. People often call this "moving the goalposts". An example can be found in the evolution of Hong Kong's Mass Transit Railway Corporation (Tang, 1995) where the major activity for almost a decade was the construction and engineering of tracks and trains. Once built, and ready for customers, business activities changed to emphasize customer service, the construction side being changed to maintenance. Engineering and construction values were very different to customer service values. The former mindset respected and valued precision and accuracy. The latter required empathy and understanding. The organization recognized this, built a successful human resource strategy and achieved cultural change.

In the case of foreign invested enterprises within the Chinese setting, culture is one of the areas that can greatly impact upon acceptance of foreign methodologies by the Chinese partner and vice versa. Values and beliefs will provide spectacles through which members will interpret organizational life. Figure 4 shows the typical activities that are involved in the internationally recognized traditional business strategy formulation process. Often the process will start with a situational audit. Next the internal and external environments are scanned to see what opportunities and threats are out in the marketplace. These are discussed and evaluated and gradually brought to a short list of priorities or strategic choices. Once generated, these are tested for fit against those environmental impacts that could make one more attractive than the other.

At this point, corporate culture (and in the case of foreign invested enterprises, the national culture that predominates in the workforce) comes in to play. Culture is so strongly pervasive and tacit that, once embedded as a set of assumptions and patterns of behavior, it is difficult to change. Culture is based on values that provide anchors to guide people through the events of the day. Decisions need to be made that harmonize with what the organization stands for, the 'who we are' element.

The case of an organizational value of quality is a good example. Should a strategy of cost minimization through 'cutting corners' be adopted with such a value in place, then there would be a values/strategy clash. It is always easier to change the strategy than the culture as the former is relatively superficial and accessible. In figure 4, imagine that the planning process yielded three major strategies. Important constraints within the environment would be set against these to see which ones would stand up best across the range of environmental variables.

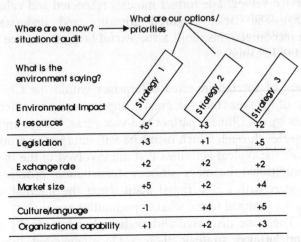

*Scoring exercise on the basis of discussion and available data
+5= most attractive: -5 least attractive

Figure 4. Strategic Planning Process

In figure 4, the third strategy has stood up better than the second strategy because there is a better cultural match. This sort of matching gives a particularly operational application to organizational vision, the outward statement of culture. For a strategy to be effectively implemented it needs to be benchmarked to organizational values. In many cases, this is achieved during the strategic planning process as environmental impact analysis.

Whatever the outcome, with human resource directors as part of the business planning process, the task of translating the chosen scenario into strategies for adoption and commitment from the workforce rests with the human resource strategist. Transmitting is not the same as translating. In the case of the chosen strategy, an accompanying education and communication strategy is required. The purpose is to develop, encourage, and educate people to the goals and methods attached to the new strategy.

The human resource strategies of FIEs operating in China need to take into account the Chinese management context, the Western context, current developments in China in relation to the distribution of labor, the state of the labor force, and ideas on China's utilization of investment. Discussion on these issues will center on a model, constructed from the 1997 study, that differentiates various approaches to human resource management. Suggested characteristics of the three approaches are shown below (Table 1).

Fundamental (Reactive)	Transitional (Tactical)	Sophisticated (Strategic)
HR a functional department	HR aware of strategy	HR strategic role
Not promotion conscious	One promotional ladder	Multiple levels/ladders
People a production cost	Cost but also an asset	Contribute to success
Short term view	Looking ahead a little	Long term view
Reacts to sales/production	Plans but tactical	HR Strategic Plan
Managers developed for job	Job plus change skills	Developed for change
Control Systems	Some autonomy	Participative systems
Taught solutions	Simple problem solving	Empowered solutions
Hierarchy of accountability	Constructive feedback	Mutual accountability
Independent function	Interconnected functions	Integrated functions
Contractual	Developmental	Continuously improve
Fragmented	Episodic	Holistic

Table 1. Characteristics of the three HR Strategies or Approaches

Adapted from Whiteley et al., 1997, interview findings

A central need and challenge for the human resource manager is the development of strategic human resource management, which in the PRC case, needs to harmonize with Chinese culture. The concept of strategic Human Resource Management outlined below (Table 2) has been well developed by both business schools and leading organizations.

Business Activities	Assessment of the Product Market
Business Activities	Adoption of Competitive Strategy
Human Resource Management Activities	Adoption of Integrated HR strategy
Human Resource Management Activities	Design systems, knowledge/skills mix
Human Resource Management Activities	Align with competitive business strategy
Human Resource Management Activities	Manage the Change Process for Present and future adaptability

Table 2. Concept of Strategic Human Resource Management

Adapted from Kitay, J. and Lansbury R. Human Resource Management and Industrial Relations in an era of Global Markets: Australian and international Trends. *Human resource management and workplace change: Proceedings of an EPAC roundtable held in Canberra on 6 February 1995.* Canberra, EPAC, Australian Government Publishing Service, p 30, 1995.

Several prerequisites are needed for the strategic human resource approach to become realized in practice. These begin with a senior management view of the centrality of the human resource role to the achievement of the competitive business strategy. This can be ascertained by the inclusion of senior human resource managers in the company's business planning and implementation strategies. Having been part of the planning process, there is the need to develop human resource strategies for producing and enhancing management and workforce skills within a long-term strategic time frame. This will involve manpower (human resource) planning and identifying which generic skills and qualities the organization needs, so that swift product changes can be absorbed. The concept requires interdependent performance, training/development and reward systems so that people are motivated, rewarded and also challenged. With an integrated system, changes can not be made in isolation since a change in one part will affect the other. This means that the strategic human resource manager will need to take a holistic view of the organization.

The real test of a strategic rather than tactical and reactive approach to human resource management is what happens in practice. Are the practised human resource management activities of a fundamental, transitional or sophisticated nature? In other words, is human resource management seen as performing the basic functions of recruiting, training and paying people? Is it involved in activities that will encourage commitment, designing the functions to reflect organizational goals and values or is it developing a whole organization that is harnessed to the business strategy? In the case of FIEs in the PRC, there is an additional aspect to consider. That is the PRC context, incorporating as it already does, strong and well developed relational business practices. This context becomes more evident with an understanding of the types of models developed in the West in relation to human resource strategy.

Fundamental Personnel Management Model

The fundamental personnel management model was heavily influenced by the scientific management movement that swept the US and other Western countries during the time of industrialization.

> *...a mechanistic outlook stresses the absolute, the unchanging and the uncertain. Ambiguity is its enemy. It stresses hierarchy, looks for isolated, separate and interchangeable parts and structures existing according to ever-descending units of analysis... So, if you add together Finance, Production, Marketing, Human Resources, Administration etc. you will have a picture of the organization (Whiteley et al., 1997:5).*

We saw earlier that 'scientific management', pioneered by Taylor (1929), had several definable characteristics that impacted on the way people were managed. First was the engineering metaphor, which, in the age of mass production, came to be applied as a mindset or paradigm (Morgan, 1980). Concerns of objectivity, efficiency, and linearity, so necessary to the synchronization and smooth running of machinery, were applied to the 'running' of people as well as machines. Just as machines were a cost to the enterprise, so were the people who operated and administered them (Wallace, 1998). Personnel were on the cost and not asset side of the organizational balance sheet. Efficient use of costly mental qualities such as 'thinking' were separated from cheaper, physical 'doing' activities. This resulted in two classes of employee: managers who did the thinking and workers who obeyed. This was an obedience model with an assumption that people would give up personal discretion for financial rewards. People (or personnel) were utilized tactically rather than strategically and were factored into the productivity equation in the most cost-saving way.

To support this selective use of workers' capabilities, control systems needed to be put in place, systems that proved so seductive that it could be argued that they became part of the productivity culture. In fact, control was the pivot around which the mechanism of management revolved. Managerial and machine control systems pervaded every aspect of the productivity process. Control systems replaced any self-control the employee might exercise as well as discretion or judgements that might alter the carefully calibrated work tasks. It was the age of instructions, taught solutions and impersonality. Relational activities were kept to a minimum and where they were absolutely necessary, were carefully prescribed and controlled. Every foreseeable contingency was met by standing operating procedures (SOPs) and instructions that required compliance. These related to tasks, relationships, reporting lines, rewards, discipline and personal relations in the workforce.

Obedience and compliance made sure that the 'cogs and wheels' meshed in an orderly fashion and human activities were assumed to follow mechanistic rules. A hallmark of the fundamental model was the assumption that the human at work was a rational economic being, best rewarded financially and organized so that human variations were replaced by machine consistency. Effective management would emphasize demarcation of authority, jobs and tasks, top-down decision making, and problem solving. The lower down the hierarchy, the simpler the decisions allowed, the less discretion and judgement permitted and the less time span expected for the job or task (Jaques, 1989).

Activities within the fundamental personnel model included induction, rather than socialization; instruction rather than coaching; inspection rather than continuous improvement; financial rather than holistic rewards, and the use of discipline rather than learning. Important management systems were technical and instructional. Monitoring and other systems involved inspection and control. In this fundamental model, the employee would be tied to the organization in a simple 'pay for work' relationship. There would be no need for a trust-building environment or any relational activities. The role of the personnel manager would be largely concerned with administration, keeping records, clarifying policies and instructions, recruiting, arranging training, and computing wages. Indeed, before the personnel function developed strategically, it very much resembled the fundamental model in spirit as well as practice.

In the 1997 research findings, there was a disparity between what was perceived in terms of sophistication (integrated human resource strategies, developmental activities, long term human resource planning) and what it was possible to achieve within the Chinese human resource framework. This was especially so in the provinces. In practice there were more fundamental indicators than sophistication ones. The actual human resource activities practiced were reported as functional, self contained and still heavily influenced by departmental requests. They were characterized by short term, ad-hoc responses rather than long term integrated planning. This was not always recognized by Foreign Invested Enterprises and therefore, rather than actively designing for a transitional period, a jump was made to sophisticated methodologies.

Transition to the Human Resource Management Model

The origins of HRM can be traced to the 1950's, in the writings of work humanist theorists such as Herzberg, Maslow and the Tavistock studies on workplace reform, and management writers such as Drucker. It came to prominence in the United States in the 1970's [attributed to] the change in competitive climate...new technologies and rising levels of educational attainment (Kitay and Lansbury 1995:21).

Continuing the theme of personnel management's transition, obedience and compliance did not encourage creativity and accountability in the face of increased competition. 'Motives' were discovered to make a difference to performance - in some cases making more of a difference than pay. These ideas and earlier findings (Roethlisberger, et al., 1939) became linked to the idea of the worker as someone with special human properties. These could be harnessed to enhance productivity and profitability, with the propensity for the worker to become an asset to the organization rather than a cost. An irony began to develop. As the ability to design better, more accurate, more detailed and standardized control systems increased, the ability or willingness of workers to be controlled decreased.

The notion of socio-technical systems in the workplace, centering around the *relationships and interactions between* technical and social structures, systems, and processes, became firmly established (Emery, 1993). Comparative theories of work were produced and were tested in the workplace. Personnel management became recognized as potentially more than a 'repository of knowledge' function, and various tools and techniques for attracting, motivating, rewarding and retaining staff were developed. Gradually, personnel management activities moved from an administrative focus to a tactical and then to a strategic focus. By around the late 1980's, David Guest was defining Human Resource Management as "the integration of human resources into strategic management and the emphasis on a full and positive utilization of these resources" (Guest, 1987:506).

During this formative period, the transformation from strategic to tactical, from control to relative self control, from prescribed to participative job designs, occurred at different times in different countries (in Australia for example, this has happened relatively recently, whereas in the US and Europe participative management is well established [Covey, 1992]). New boundaries between workers and managers began to be established. Tall, hierarchical structures suddenly became passé. They were adapted to allow gradual participation of workers in decisions about work (Nankervis et al., 1996). Managers began to educate themselves and workers in areas such as empowerment, interpersonal skills and communication (Carlopio, 1997; Whetton & Cameron, 1991).

Most importantly, the traditional functions of personnel and human resource management began to become more interconnected, tied by a desire to play an important and visible part in achieving the business strategy (Legge, 1988). People began to be recruited for future as well as present potential. Broader development activities began to complement instructional training. The intention was to produce a less narrow, task-oriented view of the worker. Performance appraisal systems began to include future-oriented development and continuous improvement measures as well as the traditional past-oriented ones. Rewards began to be linked to personal aspirations regarding organizational goals as well as simple job targets.

We are reminded of the earlier comments made about the role of outside forces and the combined power of heavy investment by Governments in education, skills formation and national manpower strategies and policies. These were accompanied by an increased emphasis on high quality standards, flexibility, adaptability and creativity across all levels in the enterprise and the push of increased competition. It is clear that transition from fundamental to sophisticated approaches to human resources is not quickly or easily achieved.

It is proposed here, that a transitional period, with gradual changes from control to commitment management strategies, is a necessary part of the journey from fundamental to sophisticated human resource management. Combined efforts of government, educators, professional institutes and enterprises will be needed to produce the environment, the intellect, and the resources to support the sort of major transition that will propel the Chinese workforce into the sophisticated model.

Internally, enterprises wishing to install human resource management in an environment in which control has been a strong feature (such as the State Owned Enterprise human resource management context [Wood, et al., 1999)] will face a firmly embedded. prescribed reality and compliance/control ethic. Very few, if any, of our FIE case organizations compared the current situation in China with the Western transitional period. It is easy to forget, once sophistication is achieved, that the transition needs to be gradual. That is not to say that now strategies, policies and procedures have been developed, tried and tested, that the process will take as long as the pioneering West. However, the pace needs to be in tune with the rate of change possible, given the particular educational and experiental history of the Chinese workforce.

Sophisticated Human Resource Management Model

This model evolved from the fundamental and transitional models of human resource management. Moving from a 'control to participation' and 'compliance to commitment' mindset was an important part of the transformation. The concept of mutuality, (Kitay et al., 1995) describes the sophisticated model well.

> *This involves a change based on management attempts to gain control over the workforce to get them to do management's bidding, one in which all employees are committed to organizational goals in an atmosphere of mutuality (Kitay et al., 1995:27).*

Another important transition was from the *short term* to the *long term* view of the worker. For this the worker needed to be considered as an asset, rather than a variable cost. In particular, the notion of *sophisticated* means negotiating for human resources to be accepted at the business strategy level. As discussed earlier, the task of strategic human resource is to enable the business strategy. To do this the human resource function must itself develop a strategy for integrating all human resource activities so that they are flexible and responsive to organizational needs.

Because of fast changing products and markets, the environment facing human resource managers is characterized more by paradox and uncertainty than congruence and certainty. The challenge today lies in the ability to provide a coherent framework of values and strategies, linked to the choice of competitive business strategy in such a way as to optimize business options through an able, adaptable and committed workforce. Guest (1987) identifies four components of the strategic human resource management model which are useful in testing the model in use discussed earlier. These are integration, commitment, flexibility/adaptability and quality.

It needs to be remembered however that some of these components may have been conceived in the Western way. The dimensions themselves may well be able to be considered as universally necessary for a strategic human resource model in use. However, the sorts of integration, as well as interpretations of terms like "flexible and adaptable behavior", may well be subject to the assumptions about allowable behavior that underpin the Chinese culture.

Integration in a strategic human resource sense means designing a whole organization to meet the ever-present challenge of change in the marketplace. Those FIEs interviewed who adopted a sophisticated approach were in agreement about which major human resource functions needed to be integrated. Recruitment, selection and retention, orientation into organizational culture, training and development combined with human resource and succession planning, performance appraisal with long term assessment criteria and appropriately designed reward systems formed a cornerstone of activities.

The identifying features of sophisticated human resource management are: a position of centrality in the organization, usually conveyed by a presence in the boardroom as a part of the business strategy formulation team; consideration of the human resource as an asset rather than a cost; association with long-term as opposed to short-term strategies; a perception of human resources as necessary to successful business performance (not only through productivity enhancement but through the strategic use of the human as opposed to technical resource); and involvement as major strategists of change and transformation.

Given the relatively recent opportunities for FIEs to develop their long term strategies and practices in China, a high preponderance of transitional arrangements and plans would be expected. In the 1997 study, however, there was a hint that FIEs thought they had managed to install sophisticated strategies and practices. The figures in the 1996 report (14% strategic and development-focus human resource management, 16% strategic and internal-focus human resource management, and 71% strategic, development-focus and internal-focus human resource management) indicated that there were a significant number of organizations who intended to be in the sophisticated category. It would be doubtful, given the superstructural and infrastructural support needed, that this could be happening in practice. More importantly, while there was an assumption that this was happening, there would be little attempt to develop a transitional strategy.

Human Resource Strategy findings

So far we have looked at some of the theory surrounding human resource strategy, as well as several models of human resource management. In this final section we discuss some of the actual findings regarding the types of human resource strategies used by organizations in Hong Kong and in China.

The significant feature of the reported human resource strategy findings in the 1997 study was that given the diverse types of business and industries, there were easily discernible common threads amongst the enterprises. In all cases there was a long term strategy able to be clearly expressed in terms of implementation and specific practices. There was shared agreement that the human resource was a valued asset, as extracts from quotations show (the symbol // separates each quotation) –

staff are the most valuable assets of the company // [we are in a] business partnership with staff".

Apart from one or two cases, there was a clear and intentional link between the business strategy and the human resource strategy.

"[we] directly link human resource strategies with [our mission] // the human resource plan is linked to the company's business strategy // human resource plan is closely linked to the business plan // [our] business strategy is to win in the product market, the people market and the financial market.

Common to all cases was a recognition of the importance of corporate culture, with the vision or values or human resource philosophy stated.

We should note that there was a range of human resource strategies actually used. To some extent there seemed to be a correlation between the perceived maturity of the workforce and the degree of control exercised over activities like policy making and decision making. However, in most cases, a participative approach was used. There was a great emphasis on facilitation and teamwork and almost all cases showed some integration of the human resource policies and activities with business goals. A Hospital organization in Hong Kong (which was often seen as a role model for the PRC) provided a good example of such an integrated human resource strategy as this extract from one in-depth interview shows.

[Our] human resources strategy is based on six broad goals. Each of these goals is supported by a set of more specific objectives, and each of the objectives has a supporting program that details how it is to be achieved. The strategy is publicised through newsletters and an orientation program for new staff, and its central tenets are built into all training programs.

The organization went on to describe the following objectives:

Directly link human resource strategies and programs to the achievement of the mission:

- Make human resource policies an integral part of the corporate plan. Ensure that the HR objectives and programs are in line with the organization's goals.

- Keep hospital management informed of the HR philosophy and strategy and encourage their feeling of involvement in them.

- Decentralize the HR function to the hospital level and empower line managers to carry out a human resources role.

- Facilitate positive changes by fostering the development of a corporate culture conducive to total quality service.

Value employees as the organization's most important assets:

- Focus the recruitment strategy on hiring the best available talent.

- Treat other staff members with the respect given to clients.

- Invest in a competitive remuneration package.

- Value professional and team contributions.

- Reward performance and achievement.

- Recognize loyalty.
- Fully utilize employees' abilities.
- Manage manpower resources.

Create an environment within which staff can fulfil their potential:
- Provide a comprehensive training and development strategy.
- Identify career paths within and across all occupational groups.
- Develop a performance-driven staff development strategy.
- Provide incentives for staff to further their own development.
- Encourage staff to participate in the decision-making process.

Foster open communications and co-operation:
- Spread the corporate mission, culture and values to all staff.
- Enhance the manager-staff relationship.
- Reinforce team building among departments and staff groups.
- Establish and reinforce channels of communication and encourage participation

  in the communication process.

Treat all staff fairly and equitably:
- Establish fair and equitable HR policies and procedures.
- Promote consistent management practices.

Treat each individual with respect and dignity:
- Value staff opinions. Line managers are consulted over the first draft of any HR

  plans and feedback is sought from the different professions, such as doctors and

  nurses.
- Demonstrate concern and care for individual staff members.
- Respect the individual and the profession he or she represents.

A comment on this case, which was fairly indicative of both public sector and large (not Chinese family-owned) enterprises, is that right up to the 1996 and 1997 studies, Hong Kong ostensibly shared many of the benefits and philosophical foundations of Western-evolved human resource management. There was a powerful expatriate presence during the time that

Hong Kong was a crown colony. It was during this time that the 'personnel-to-human resource management' conceptual framework developed. Some of the responses such as the final objective above that single out the individual would not be in keeping with the group and social harmony ideals that are so clearly a desired part of Chinese life. Although this syndrome was not specifically studied for this book, we can surmise that even when there was a 'professional individual' to be talked about, some adaptation would be made to preserve groupness and the collective face.

Hong Kong enterprises operating in the PRC

The human resource strategies of the Hong Kong companies operating in the PRC were less integrated than the Hong Kong operations, and yet more integrated than the PRC-based companies. The following quotation (from a hi-tech organisation with a workforce of "young talent" and skilled people) shows recognition of the importance of the human resource.

the business units develop business programs. With the knowledge of the business strategies, it is HR's job to enhance performance of staff, to make sure of manpower, to recruit, to develop training and to retain staff in order to meet the business needs.

In a labor intensive manufacturing enterprise the picture was a little different.

the HR Director in HK set up a model (same as HK) for the PRC plant to follow and develop. Mr X took a very rigid position but used a mild and popular manner to convince the heads of HR of the PRC plants to adopt the HR policies and practices set up by the HK side.

The following quotes were from conglomerates with a strong group position.

Effective human resources management and development are key factors in business success. The Corporation emphasizes the use and development of internal human resources, through its Philosophy in staff recruitment and training and its carefully planned staff training and development plans/schemes. The most important factor for the corporate to consider is the mentality of persons. It explains that the corporation choose only those persons with virtue/moral integrity but not those without moral

*integrity even if they possess good working abilities. It emphasizes the importance of
a person's virtue over that of ability.*

*The company has always adopted a global approach which encouraged staff to be
transferred worldwide to strengthen their know-how and understanding its
worldwide operation. The company valued employees' sense of participation and
involvement in the company, as well direct and straightforward communication with
employees. In the meeting held by the chairman (monthly or bi-monthly meeting),
even the tea lady was invited to join and raise concerns. Opinion surveys were also
used to facilitate communication between the management and employees. As quoted
by Mr X, "that is the soft issue to make the success".*

The next quotation characterized the "HK in the PRC" position on
rewarding performance. Almost all cases took the 'reward for performance'
approach, although they were not, overall, as comprehensive as the "HK in
HK" cases. An interesting point to note was that there were some differences
between the performance infrastructure set up and the corresponding
practices achieved in the PRC.

*Promoting communication between staff, retention of staff of good quality (as it was
difficult to recruit high quality of staff from the market and it was to avoid the
outflow of HR investment of the company) and pay strictly by performance were the
main strategies adopted by the company.*

Sometimes an HR function was a dominant activity - this was closer to
the type claimed as HR strategies by the PRC-based enterprises.

*The HR strategies are mainly focused on staff training. The Training Committee has
been set up for 8 months with the objective to monitor the training policies and plans
of the company in the region and have quarterly meetings. The members are the
representatives from various regions (including Hong Kong, PRC and other
countries) who are at the senior to top management level.*

Overall, there was a 'parental' impression to the HR strategies employed
in the PRC. Well-defined sets of transitional strategies aimed at moving
workers from the heavily controlled to the self-controlled systems indicative
of the sophisticated approach were not so evident. There were some PRC
cases in which the level of integration achieved was similar to those in Hong

Kong and elsewhere. The integration in these cases was well-established, with cases typically not labor intensive and manufacturing.

PRC-based Foreign Invested Enterprises

There were three very evident types of human resource strategy in the PRC. One was an outcome of the business strategy of investing to take advantage of low-cost labor. Not surprisingly, this corresponded to the *fundamental* approach reactive to a short term cost based situation.

The human resource strategy was clearly differentiated between managers and workers and any human resource investment was made in the management group. Production, sales and other functions operated independently, simply informing the "human resource department" of requests for labor whilst doing on-the-job training for task related activities themselves. Typically there was a material method of motivating such as contracts or bonus incentives. For managers there would be a variety of technical and management development activities of a tactical rather than strategic nature. In this type, the view was that either labor turnover and poor performance did not matter because there was plenty of labor available or that the product/service was so elementary that it did not require high performance. When asked for the human resource strategy such enterprises gave functional activities as their version of human resource strategy.

The main function of the Personnel Department is to serve the employees. The Department also handles recruitment. Some of the employees were recruited from the local parent company before the joint venture, the rest were recruited later. With regards to salary, the General Manager issues an instruction to the Personnel Department which includes the maximum number of employees and the proportional work force of the two production lines.

Four of the Company's strategies are related to staff. It is obvious that the Company has certain expectations in the human resources area, the minimum forty hours training policy, the localization of staff, that the employees are encouraged to discuss their future plans with their superiors, and that efforts are made to employ the most talented people are illustrations of this. If new staff are required, the department head will submit a request to the Human Resource Department. The Human

Resource Department will then interview, select and recruit the new staff. It will also organize training for new employees

The second type of human resource strategy approximated the developmental type strategy. In these cases, human resources may not have been integrated with the business strategy but the value of the human resource was clearly discernible.

The Personnel Department is busy in managing personnel matters, it is not therefore involved in formulating Company strategy. The most important human resource strategy is training and development. The training program is designed in accordance with the need of the industry. The company serves foreign tourists. The sales staff are required to speak good English and Japanese. They also need to have professional knowledge... This requires training. The Company is very concerned about the stability of the work force. In order to stabilize the work force, especially the high proportion of "Chih Ts'ing" (educated young people), the Company launched a cohesion framework. This year, the "Chih Ts'ing" Children Society is formed and an adviser is assigned for every four to five "Chih Ts'ing" children.

In some of these cases, the human resource function was not part of the start-up organisational design. This could be because the enterprise was small, as below, or because it was newly formed.

As the Company is relatively small, the Human Resources Department is more like an administrative office. There are two employees in the Personnel Department and it is their duty to oversee general affairs, deal with personnel matters and give support to different departments. Recruitment is carried out by several agencies...

The third type, accounting for less than a quarter of the respondents, involved an integrated HR strategy. The enterprises belonging to this type were not all hi-tech/young talent organisations. One was in a service industry renowned for turnover and performance problems. One was labor intensive manufacturing and another (quoted below) manufactured health products. There were enterprises within those studied whose circumstances were not dissimilar but who did not invest in a strategic human resource management approach.

The human resources strategy serves the business and production plans, it is therefore based upon the company strategy and production goals. The strategies are made after the general strategy and production goals have been formulated. At the Company, human resources are considered to be the greatest asset. Every employee is important, regardless of his position in the company hierarchy. Teamwork is valued and efforts are made to create pleasant working conditions for all members of staff. Stabilizing the workforce is one of the main goals of the Human Resources Department. Much extra work is done by the Department in the areas of recruitment, training, management and improving welfare benefits. Efforts are made to help the employees to adjust to the changing economic environment and to make the Company "the best place for the most outstanding individuals".

The issue of human resource strategy in China is a complex issue. The so-called discipline of human resource management can not be isolated from the societal and management philosophies lying underneath major social institutions of which organizations are one. In transporting organizations and designs, only the edifice of activities such as structures, systems and processes can be moved. Even then these are designed to be in harmony with the structural functional sociology of the West (Putnam, 1993). Similarly, although it would be possible and achievable to adopt the titles and some of the functional activities above, these would form the edifice and could only work if placed on the appropriate foundations (figure 5).

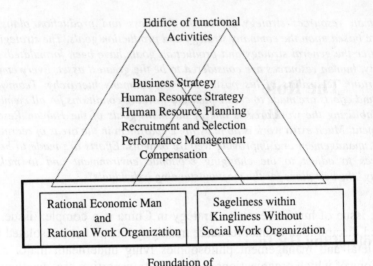

Edifice of functional
Activities

Business Strategy
Human Resource Strategy
Human Resource Planning
Recruitment and Selection
Performance Management
Compensation

Rational Economic Man and Rational Work Organization	Sageliness within Kingliness Without Social Work Organization

Foundation of
Philosophy of Business and Society

Figure 5. New Foundations Needed

As we go on to look at the findings on human resource practices, these foundational issues need to be borne in mind. Thinking about Nankervis's (1999) comments on strategic human resource management (SHRM) and Tyson's (1995) comments on the roles of human resource practitioners, it is very clear that special interpretation is needed for these to be desirable and relevant in China.

5. The Role of the HR Function in Foreign Invested Enterprises

The role of the HR function in Foreign Invested Enterprises

Singapore's recognition of the importance of the human resource (as described by Torrington et al. (1994:15) could have been written about the Chinese aspiration (Cheng, et al., 1995). Singapore's government demonstrated the intention to integrate selected aspects of social and economic policies with foreign practices. Like China, it recognized that human resources could play an important role in achieving prosperity. In this chapter and the next, we explore the role of the human resource department in FIEs and look more closely at several human resource functions, including training and development of staff, recruitment and selection, compensation and retention, and performance appraisal. With information from Hong-Kong invested PRC-based enterprises and other PRC-based FIEs, we explore current practices and future opportunities.

The development of human resource management from a Western perspective was described in earlier chapters. A central theme in this development was that the HR function was perceived as critical to organizational success, with people considered more as autonomous decision-makers than as passive, compliant followers. People were encouraged to be empowered, committed, involved and resourceful (Torrington, et al., 1994). Such a role evolved toward complexity, frequently involving senior executives, especially when changing mission or organizational strategies. Integration, or the taking of a long-term view, became the hallmark of a well-developed human resource management

115

function. Within such integration was a developmental and potential-conscious approach (rather than purely a performance approach).

However, findings from our 1997 study showed that such integration might not have yet arrived in many FIEs. In their China operations, a moment's reflection would give some idea as to why this might be. Several studies have reported the potential conflicts inherent in the foreign partner/Chinese partner relationship. Almost every aspect of the business deal, from contract negotiations through to human resource management can show incongruencies. This can be due (amongst other factors) to language and cultural differences, an inability to tailor policy and process to the local environment, differing perspectives as to the nature of the business relationship and the purpose of the enterprise. In some cases there are problems of control and ownership of resources. Some of the incongruencies uncovered in our research were transparent and easier to harmonize, given the experience of many foreign partners in adapting to other cultures. Some incongruencies however, would not harmonize. The Chinese setting was seen as particularly vulnerable to the situation of disharmony due to these incongruencies. A case example showed differences in the acceptable method of performance appraisal feedback. This made it difficult for the subordinate to tell a Chinese manager that s/he was doing a bad job (a Western responsibility felt by most workers). Western managers, especially confident, sophisticated people, expected "360-degree feedback" (Carless, Mann, & Wearing, 1998) where many social rules and norms would be automatically infringed here.

From our 1996 and 1997 research, a popular model of operation in enterprises appeared to be one in which business strategy for the PRC operation was developed by business units, often located in other regions (for example, Hong Kong). For Hong Kong enterprises operating in the PRC the following quotation was indicative of responses about the way PRC operators connected HR to the business.

HR involvement as in the boardroom meeting is not enough. It is probably one or two steps behind in the business line. Nevertheless HR has already taken an advisory role concerning business in the PRC. For example, before starting negotiation with a prospective PRC partner, HR advises where new plant should be located, where people with the right skills can be found and trained, how to communicate with the PRC partners, what is the implication of taking a certain proportion of PRC staff.

In two participating cases, the human resource manager was considered as a business partner, with the human resource operating as a strategic function. In one case the human resource function was involved in business strategies on a case by case basis. There was agreement that human resource managers (in some cases this meant line managers who were responsible for human resources) needed to know the business strategies.

What role then should human resource managers take? Responses from actual FIEs included: balancing the cultures of Joint Venture and PRC organizations, providing people, spotting potential, understanding and interpreting the law and liaising with such agencies as government employment agencies. Such findings are supported by recent research by Bjorkman and Lu (1999), who note the development of 'China Centers' – centralized, China-based offices which co-ordinate the HR functions to the various enterprises within China. The development of the China Center may be one way in which FIEs are coming to terms with the diverse role of human resource managers within the Chinese setting.

Various ways to define the role of human resource in PRC-based FIEs are possible. Our research however, reveals three key roles. These are *administrative, personnel management* and *strategic* human resources and are largely in keeping with the findings of other researchers. For example, Nicholson International (1998:30) suggests that the field of human resources in China is still developing and focuses heavily on personnel and administration – due to a legacy of the Communist cradle-to-grave system of caretaking. In our research however, the administrative category did not even cover the basic personnel activities, and personnel management activities were often more directed than managed (see table 1).

Administrative: administered basic activities such as recruitment

record keeping, training in company rules, compute salary

Personnel management: linked PM activities to company goals in a limited way.

Waited for directions to recruit, arranged training designed or managed some

management development activities. Linked performance to rewards. Developed

---

retention strategies. Control systems in place with formalized
instructions. Carried out administrative tasks. Worked with other depts.

Strategic HR: Designed HR strategy to enable business plan. Long term view of the
human resource. Plans transformed into HR policies and practices. Use of
management models. Succession conscious and developmental approach.

Integrated: in the sense of being involved with the development of business strategy.
Holistic view of the organisation and a role in the design and management of change
processes

Table 1. The role of HR in PRC-based FIEs

Adapted from Whiteley, et al., 1997, interview findings)

Human Resource Practices

We said earlier that our 1996 study found that the most important and
challenging PRC practices in the next three years were to include major
human resource functions. Most of these were again highlighted in our 1997
interviews. Practices involving cultural differences were considered as
critical. The next sections of this chapter deal with these practices
individually, beginning with management development and training.

Management Development

Nowhere in human resource management does the history of Western
management so overtly demonstrate the results of decades of evolution than
in the case of management development. In particular, a look at the core
management development concepts in Carlopio (1997), adapted from
Whetton and Cameron's longstanding work in this area (Whetton et al.,
1991), illustrates the centrality of the concept of personal development to
management development theory.

The Western concept of personal skills development includes many expressions of personal self awareness that are a function of the management style journey from regulation and control, to autonomy and participative management development. Self-awareness is a cornerstone of Whetton et al.'s management development process. Emphasis is placed very much on the notion of self - "students of human behavior have long known that knowledge of oneself – self-awareness, self-insight, self-understanding is essential to one's productive personal and interpersonal functioning and empathizing with other people" (Carlopio, 1997:64).

Carlopio (and Whetton) represent Western management development orthodoxy when they describe four areas of self-awareness – personal values, cognitive style, attitude to change and interpersonal orientation. Conceptually, these become the pillars of the all-important 'self-concept'. *Personal values* (rather than social values) define an individual's standards about what is good and bad, right and wrong and an individual's standpoint on other moral issues. The concept of *cognitive style* describes the way people individually process and interpret information. This often involves moral judgements. *Attitude to change* is also regarded as a personal matter with individuals seeing themselves as future looking, happy to operate in uncertainty and adaptable, or in contrast conservative, preferring certainty and structure. *Interpersonal orientation* is also largely a function of how a person wants to see him/herself. This can equally well be as a retiring and self-conscious person or as an assertive and socially conscious individual. The self-concept in this instance is not related to the social self. The Western manager, for example, may fear losing self-respect, but not social respect, unlike the Chinese counterpart.

A glance at some of the concepts in these areas reinforces the difference in approach (Western and Chinese) that accompanies such management activities as managing stress, solving problems, communicating, gaining power and influence, managing conflict and building effective teams. From a Western approach, central to managing stress are personality inventories that help tell the person whether s/he is intense and hard driving or more relaxed and accepting (Cacioppe & Mock, 1985). A central part of problem solving is fostering the (unnatural) ability to deal with ambiguity and uncertainty rather than with precision and regulation. Western-style communication skills focus on making sure that people learn 'win-win' approaches, that cooperation has great benefits, that other points of view need to be taken into account as well as one's own, and that communication is better couched in the positive than the negative. These concepts are already an embedded part of the Chinese culture, yet they are often re-learned in a different norm framework from that employed in the Western setting. Ling, Chen, & Wang (1987) for example, point to a moral character dimension of leadership not evident in Western leadership research.

In the West, an effective management development program would most probably display some of the following elements. The program would be integrated with the performance management of the individual. Development would be principally in three areas: generic, leadership skills and complex problem solving as related to a particular professional area. Rewards would be inter-related with work performance and developmental achievements. For those marked as senior management potential there would be broadening experiences such as being located overseas or in another industry. If the enterprise could sustain it, there would be multiple career paths. A competency framework would include competencies in knowing the business, successful transmission of the organization's vision, mission and strategies to others, creativity, innovation and those competencies connected with 'achieving through others'.

In the Chinese setting, although these headings still apply, there is a very definite overlay necessary for achieving 'development with a feeling of comfort'. Although recent research indicates a turn in China towards many of the individualistic activities associated with management development including career planning and individual salaries, human resource activities such as (for example) managerial selection are nevertheless influenced far more by social relationships than in the West at least overtly. Some of the Chinese social and personal conventions and responsibilities have already been discussed and these appear to take precedence over some of the more individualistic, less socially oriented developmental activities.

In the 1996 and 1997 studies, as well as in a study by Wood, et al. (1999), the view was put forward that overall, China does not have enough well-trained people, the main issue therefore being to identify potential staff with an aim to localize PRC managers. Localization of managerial staff is a key issue for FIEs (Wong & Law, 1999). From our research it was particularly evident that those organizations in computer-related or other hi-tech industries were very worried about the link between a need to constantly update and innovate product, and the knowledge that business could double or triple in a short time. A key strategy here was to encourage employees to take a long-term view and to provide comprehensive management training and development accompanied by an attractive compensation package. Enterprises wanted to hire graduates - the feeling was that only the graduates from the best PRC universities were better than those in Hong Kong, since otherwise PRC graduates were not as good. This sentiment has been widely expressed in the research literature and is also a key reason for the Chinese government's educational push, and the development of initiatives such as the Shanghai Business Leadership 2000 programme (Ko, 1998).

Some organizations had their own core program and here *"managers were to handle various projects with the objective to offer themselves opportunities to move out or move up"*. Programs were typically of two to three years duration and covered such areas as foundation of management training, performance and development review, management of change (including the use of computer, management style and change of concept of the fresh graduates) productivity and skill range.

[Our] Management Trainee Training Programme is a three-year training programme. Successful staff who complete the programme will be promoted to the junior and middle management levels. Basically, the programme materials are quite similar to that used in Hong Kong, except some modifications like more training on English comprehension which are provided in the PRC. To evaluate effectiveness of the training programme, the senior management meets the trainees quarterly to solicit their feedback and assess what they have learnt from the training.

One major developmental focus was on orienting managers to the ways of the parent enterprise (which was typically not Chinese) and on improving English as the business language. It was in this function that one can see a bridge built between two very different management styles at work, Western and Chinese. Examples such as the one below also indicate that communication is a key factor. However, in our research there were few explicit descriptions of how Chinese values were harmonized with foreign values or how foreign values and other messages were diffused to supervisors and workers, even though, as Antoniou and Whitman (1998) suggest, one reason for problems related to cultural differences can be found in a lack of understanding of the values held by the representative of the Chinese partner and the Chinese work force. There was also reference to the need that "the mentality of local PRC staff should be changed in order to enhance customer service and management" and throughout our interviews the need for change was seen as a change in line with FIE outlooks and arrangements.

Communication of staff between various locations of staff in the PRC was highly emphasised and was supported by the top management. The Staff News Committee was set up to publish an in-house Staff Newsletter (content included activities of the company, message from top to general level of staff and other "warm" staff news). On top of this, an annual one-week training program was also arranged for all levels of staff from various operations in the PRC. Other than providing management and skills training, the main reason of this annual one-week training program is to facilitate staff from various locations to know each other and to exchange experience.

Taking communication as an example, interviewed FIEs were agreed on the need for "open communication". However, there did not seem to be any recognition of the need to link this need to the gradual building of trust and openness that would represent the Chinese foundation for developing personal relationships. Conceivably, the permissible content of open communication, particularly with superiors, would be very different. Given the 'three irons' (iron rice bowl; iron pay and iron chair) which were well entrenched as work-lore and the natural deference to superiors discussed earlier, one would expect to find much detail on cross-cultural issues in a discussion about communication. One organization reported that "*an opinion survey was also used to facilitate communication between the management and employees*". Even in the West at the grass roots level, an opinion survey often assumes more survey-sophistication than employees possess. Given the strong and effective informal networking preferences (such as guanxi), described earlier, some doubt could be cast on the 'two way-ness' of management communication through survey techniques.

A model that did seem to take into account two way-ness was the China Competency Model designed by one organization, a veteran in operating in Asia.

A 5-people task force had been set up for 18 months from different business units to set up the China Competency Model which would be applied from top, senior to middle management levels for HR planning and development. There was no time table for this model to be set up to ensure the success not hindered by time constraints. The Hay Mcber would probably be used for this model.

Under the China Competency Model in planning, an entity approach would be adopted for people development. The elements of competency to be emphasised included way of thinking and perception self management (including innovation, time management) ability to influence people and resource orientation.

Such an approach matched with the company's focus on cultivating PRC employees' teamwork concept and loyalty - indispensable elements of staff involvement especially at middle management level. The opinion was that companies in the PRC should have a long-term, people development vision and that such an approach would eventually benefit the labor market as a whole.

The findings above suggest that this is a good time to be thinking of developing a special way of harmonizing some of the traditonal Western management development activities with Chinese values and behavioral rules. In particular, an understanding of communication processes and of the general need for business education will aid in the development of local managers in FIEs. Furthermore however, such education needs to be provided in a culturally appropriate manner – this will entail in many cases a redefinition of the function of some management activities (such as appraisal and devices for communication with staff).

Staff Training

The training concept is usually expressed in terms of the three capabilities required of the trainee, that is Knowledge (cognitive skills), Attitudes (affective skills) and Skills (psychomotor skills), commonly referred to as KASs. These are typically related to a job, task or element of a task. All three areas of training are usually required in any job, although there is usually an emphasis on one or two. For example, a hotel receptionist could bring affective and knowledge components to the fore where a systems analyst might emphasize cognitive and psychomotor skills.

An effective training program can be based on job and role analysis, together with the interface or social qualities needed to support the job. Training can be toward organizational objectives, job objectives or personal objectives. A training strategy takes into account the direction of the organization so that some KAS training for the future can be incorporated into current training plans and programs. Training programs are seen as continuing only as long as they serve the business strategy, however successful they become.

Programs should include objectives, standards, desired outcomes and appropriate experience with which to achieve them. In basic tasks, training may follow 'job instruction skills'. In others, skills mastery, linked to efficacy skills, is often needed.

Once again, it is worth remembering that these descriptors have an etic quality to them. This means that the *what* will be very different from the *how*. A good example is training for self efficacy. In the Western-style, public viewing of videos is often used, so that others, including subordinates, are able to provide feedback by pointing out mistakes. Such a device in the Chinese setting, however, carries face and mianxi (that is emic) considerations. Video devices need to be more carefully managed in the Chinese setting, including, but not limited to consideration of the composition of the feedback group.

In the 1996 study, companies were asked to provide information on training with respect to policy, budget, training days, priority, reasons for training and development, methods of evaluation and their policy on sponsorship.

73.2% of the responding companies had a training and development policy. Of those companies that possessed such a policy, 51% had the policy in written form. Large companies were more likely to set a training budget than small ones. Comparing companies of different nationality of ownership, US-owned companies were more likely to set a training budget while this practice was less common in HK-owned companies.

For companies that had an annual budget, the majority were set at a level below 3% of the total staff payroll (Table 2).

Training expenditure as a % of total staff payroll	Percentag e
0 – 1%	30.1
2 – 3%	31.1
4 – 7%	22.3
8% plus	16.5

Table 2. Training Budget

Most of the responding companies (86%) supported their staff attending external courses or seminars by granting sponsorship, of which 55% paid the full fee for the staff while 17% gave half sponsorship. Overall, companies provided more training days for junior/frontline staff. However, variations between companies for the same levels of staff were substantial. In general, training and development for managerial and professional staff was considered more important than for those staff at clerical, supervisory, manual or technician levels.

There were many factors affecting the training and development activities of the case organisations. In fact, the findings here do not give the impression of a maturely developed training industry. The overall results of the 1996 survey indicated that the more important factors were "improvement of the administrative ability of management", "productivity improvement", "expansion of skill range", "development of employees' ability to cope with technical innovation", "response to product changes" and "improvement of employees' morale" (Table 3).

	Factors	Importance rating
1.	Improvement of the administrative ability of management	4.6
2.	Productivity improvement at workplace	4.4
3.	Expansion of skill range of employee	4.3
4.	Development of employees' ability to cope with technical innovation	4.2
5.	Response to product changes	4.1
6.	Improvement of employees' morale	4.1
7.	Improvement and development of working relations and cooperation between expatiates and local employees	3.9
8.	Development of new technologies	3.9
9.	Improvement of safety and hygiene	3.9
10.	Stabilisation of labour-management relationship	3.9

Table 3. Factors Shaping the Companies' Training and Development Activities

The more popular methods for evaluating training effectiveness were "obtaining feedback through questionnaires from trainees", "interview with trainees' supervisor", "information from performance appraisals of the trainees", "interview with trainers" and "observing behaviour of the trainees". The main sources of feedback came from trainees, trainers and trainees' supervisors (table 4).

	Percentage				
Method Source	Questionnaire	Interview	Observation	Performance appraisal	None
Trainees	52.5	36.9	44.7	45.4	3.5
Trainers	27.7	45.4	33.3	29.8	7.8
Trainees' supervisor	10.6	48.2	22.0	34.8	9.2
Trainees' subordinates	10.6	25.5	34.0	16.3	23.4
Trainees' clients	24.1	19.9	18.4	20.6	28.4

Table 4. Source of Information and Method of Training Effectiveness

Conglomerates were more likely to use questionnaires for trainees and to conduct interviews with the trainees' supervisors. Observation by trainees' clients was less frequently adopted by the manufacturing sector. Although interviews with trainees' subordinates was not a common method, it was more likely to be used by PRC-owned companies.

In those FIEs linked to Hong Kong stakeholders, a strong emphasis was placed on technical training since "technical training catches young people who were not shaped by the cultural revolution..."

training was provided to sales staff including overseas training... a local (HK) training officer (electronic engineer) was employed to train the local PRC workers.

Tests would be given to staff to see if they fulfil occupational requirements; if not they would be sacked".

Clearly there were some frustrations and the following statement was typical.

"The salesmen have no "client" or "consumer" concept. Sometimes they are so rude as to turn away clients. Some salesmen are quite fast in learning and they can change their mentality very quickly, and the company labels them as the "486 pentiumable model". However, an overall improvement is not expected for a few years".

Sometimes cultural sensitivity drove the training effort since "the difference in culture affects the design of training. The trainers have to give the trainee the demonstration and stories with which they are familiar to help them become familiar with the Western concept first". The detail of one company's experience is outlined below - this experience was part of a comprehensive people investment strategy.

Ours is the first company in the PRC to conduct a program which issues a formal certificate of management development performance in the PRC. In 1995, the modules of this one-year program have various focuses including time management, motivation, characteristics of managers, team work and team building. Lecturers were from the University of Hong Kong who went to PRC to conduct the modules weekly. The programme was to progress bit by bit, phase by phase in order to make sure of its effectiveness. The achievement can be demonstrated by the [company] plants who got the ISO 9000 certificates within 8 to 9 months while other companies might take years to get it.

Most organizations isolated the following items for training: coaching, staff empowerment, creating a learning environment, language training and on-job-training. The view was that "PRC nationals are eager to learn" and an organization commented that the PRC could overtake Hong Kong if it was not careful. One employer captured the spirit of the training task facing FIEs.

"In the factory, an orientation programme is designed for those newly joined so that they have an idea of how the factory operates and the rules and regulations of the plant. Later on, work training is provided. Once the technical training in place, they have induction into corporate culture and vision to educate staff to be independent,

forward thinking & creative. Staff who have the corporate ethic can work within the corporate framework.

There did seem to be some generic training tasks for FIEs, represented in this example.

Sales and marketing skills training

Management skills training (including attitude training)

Technical skills training Computer training to catch up the computerisation plan which is being conducted by 2 Hong Kong computer experts on E-mail English language training

FIEs within the PRC showed more reluctance overall to invest in the long term development of staff than did those based in Hong Kong. This may not apply as much to managers. Still, whereas in Hong Kong there was almost a taken-for-grantedness that managers would be given comprehensive development, often linked to the enterprise's succession, manpower and business plan, in the PRC this could not be taken so much for granted. There was a bigger incidence of ad-hoc on the job training in the PRC - this could be undertaken by anyone from a personnel representative to a line manager, department head or even a senior manager.

The human resources department is also responsible for staff training and development. After co-ordinating with the other departments, the human resources department will carry out suitable training courses. Training is mainly given to managerial and technical staff, and there seems to be too much concentration on training merely to improve production and not to improving the quality of the general workers.

The workers receive on the job training and once they have mastered their skills, their attitudes towards their work and observing company regulations often deteriorates. Unlike very high-tech companies, knowledge of and training in technology is not required.

There were also some examples of education and training systems that could rival those anywhere in the world.

One of the characteristics of the company is the emphasis placed upon training. In order to give every employee the opportunity to realise his potential, several million dollars have been spent on training. Interestingly, beneficial and effective courses are provided for employees at all levels. Each employee receives intensive training on his duties and safety matters. Those at management level are instructed in up-to-date management techniques. Training is also provided for specific skills such as English and computing in order that the employees will become the best in their fields. Appreciation is shown for outstanding work by sending selected employees abroad for the purposes of training and travel.

These examples, however, serve primarily to emphasize the need for coordinated training strategies within FIEs – as we shall look at next in recruitment and selection, there is a shortage of talented workers. Training and skill development of managers particularly local managers is often in conjunction with career development. These are key activities of which human resource managers must take full advantage in order to prosper in the rapidly changing Chinese business environment. Whilst some organizations are at the forefront (Motorola, for example, opened a Beijing branch of its Motorola University in 1993, [Cui, 1998]), others, like that featured in the case study below, are having to play catch-up to survive.

Case Study – A Role for Development Activities?

T.L. Electronics Company is a Japanese invested enterprise concentrating on the production of engines for computerized fabric cutters. The company has five hundred members of staff and the Japanese parent company has a number of plants in Japan. Due to the influence of the sole Japanese stakeholder, Japanese technology and management styles are used in the company. The General Manager Mr. Watanabe, was appointed in Japan. The Company also imports the majority of its production materials from Japan and all of its manufactured product is exported back to Japan – in fact, the Company was formed solely to take advantage of cheap labor in China.

According to the Chinese workers, the style of Japanese management is not conducive to Chinese expectations, for example:

- Chinese workers are employed on a two-year contract basis (normal practice in this area). The Parent company can refuse to renew a contract without giving any reason for their decision however Japanese workers are employed on permanent contract and concern is shown for their personal development
- the same management style is used for workers at all levels although attitudes to staff at various levels differ and rules are implemented in different ways; the system is more lenient on the managers than it is on the general workers
- it is not considered important for the employees to understand the Company goals as they are merely workers on short term contracts. Vertical communication is achieved through Instruction Documents that are issued by the management staff resulting in a strictly downward flow of information
- few fringe benefits (such as babysitting services) have been offered to the workforce
- housing is provided only for management staff, not general workers

In addition, misunderstandings due to language problems abound, with a distinct lack of Chinese/Japanese bi-lingual personnel. The main concern of employees remains salary with re-numeration at T.L. Electronics in the middle-range compared to other firms in the area. Outside of salary, although training is given before new employees start their jobs, no further professional development training is offered.

Previously, it has been an employers' market. This has meant few difficulties in retaining workers. Over one thousand applications were routinely received for each vacancy. Nevertheless, the Company has always experienced a high turnover rate, particularly amongst younger workers. The turnover rate is now beginning to have a worsening effect on the Company, as other FIEs move in and attract those workers with managerial experience, offering better pay rates and further training opportunities.

Q1. Why does the Japanese style of management in this example have such an impact on the Chinese workforce?

Q2. Why, do you think, is this company unwilling to invest in training for its Chinese workforce?

Q3. What can be done to reduce the worsening turnover rate amongst (particularly younger) workers in this Company?

Q4. How would some of these changes be best implemented in this environment?

Q5. Would the motivation of Japanese workers be affected if their power or conditions were eroded? What can be done to ensure this does not occur?

Recruitment and Selection

In the West, recruitment and selection is part of the organization's grand plan. The organization will design its core systems, structures and processes depending upon the way it sees itself, and this includes those processes for hiring and promotion. Overall, in the West, recruitment and selection is a function of organizational design and organizational culture. The culture of the organization will influence the patterns of behavior that will be acceptable across the range of jobs in the workplace. Organizational expectations, management style and employee relations will provide the environment within which the new recruit will find him/herself. This environment is called the job design and within the design is the sort of structuring of relationships that preserve the culture. In establishing actual employee specifications, the job is described in detail and a pen picture of a suitable person is drawn (see figure 1).

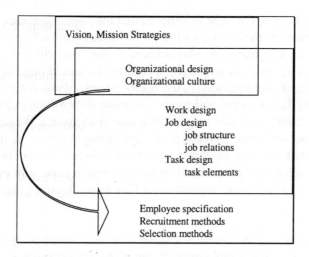

Figure 1. Recruitment & Selection in context

This is a very logical and rational approach to the recruitment and selection environment. It is in keeping with the Western rational and objective mindset described earlier in the book. The findings that follow suggest that indeed, this is the prevailing mindset. However, this approach to recruitment and selection is not necessarily shared by those working in Chinese enterprises. Nicholson International (1999) makes two pertinent points regarding this aspect of the human resource function. The first is that the focus on administration of benefits and maintenance of relationships with government bureaus that characterized the traditional human resource function in Chinese enterprise meant recruitment and selection processes were of (relatively) little concern. Second, that Chinese personnel staff had been trained to select a candidate based more on which university they graduated from than on the actual skills possessed by the graduate. Whilst in the West this has also been a complaint made of some selection procedures, Wood, et al. (1999) show that the more relational and particularistic elements of Chinese culture (such as the 'guanxi' associated with a particular institution) can be an intervening influence on what really happens in human resource processes, including recruitment and selection. It would be dangerous to believe (or want to believe) that the impersonal recruitment and selection system of the West could in fact be transported wholesale to China. A human resource manager who wanted to optimise the etic, that is the universal concept such as employee specification, would need to modify the Western emic of specification (based solely on objective job data) to include that based on the 'warmer' and more subjective dimensions in keeping with the Chinese family-oriented culture. We note that, from a Western point of view, such an approach implies a sub-optimizing element in the guise of extra resources needed to run a system within a system. However the benefits of such emic optimization should become evident with the influence provided by certain emic aspects of Chinese work performance such as guanxi.

Analysed by size of companies, there were more large companies putting notices outside their establishment's premises for recruitment than small companies.   Large companies were also more likely to use the labour department or a local employment service in recruitment. Analysed by industry, there were more companies in the manufacturing sector using the labour department or a local employment service than in other industries However, advertising in English newspapers was far less prevalent in the manufacturing sector (see table 5).

Method	Percentage
Labour department-local employment service	80.8
Personal recommendation from existing staff	70.5
Advertising in Chinese newspapers	67.3
Employment agencies/consultant	50.0
Advertising in English newspapers	23.1
Notices outside establishment's premises	14.1
Advertising in professional and trade journals	10.9
Others	15.4

Table 5. Methods of Recruitment

A look at the 1996 findings on the channels of recruitment shows that labour department or local employment agencies, personal recommendation from existing staff and advertising in Chinese newspapers were the most popular (Table 5). Reasons for these results might include those suggested by Nicholson International (1999) – that local newspaper advertisements work best for large blue-chip companies well recognised by those young professionals with 'talent', whilst networking works well for companies with some experienced local staff, and employment agencies and labor departments work well for companies unfamiliar with the Chinese environment. Interestingly, the Internet is also beginning to play a larger role in selection and recruitment, however this appears to be most useful amongst those employees comfortable with such technology.

In terms of selection, over 90% of the responding companies used selection interviews (Table 6). The majority of the companies reported that both human resource and line departments were involved and that many of them relied on one interviewer only.

Analysed by size of company, a higher proportion of large companies carried out their own test of trade knowledge/skill in the selection process. Bjorkman, et al. (1999) have pointed out however, that standardized tests used in other parts of the world can run into problems in China. They cite an example of an analytical problem-solving test used by a large US consumer goods company which screened out less than 12% of Chinese applicants, as opposed to 50% of U.S. applicants. Furthermore, psychological tests used to predict personality traits also have questionable validity if designed outside of China.

Analysed by industry, conglomerates were more likely to use application forms and to conduct reference checks. Assessment centres were used by 5% of the respondents – an interesting response given that research has shown that activities common within assessment centres such as group-based problem solving activities are likely to suffer from the relationship-orientation and hierarchical nature of cultural norms (Bjorkman et al., 1999).

Method	Percentage
Interview	92.9
Application form	77.6
Own test of trade knowledge/skill	72.4
Reference check	62.2
Physical check-up	61.5
Psychometric tests	9.0
Assessment centre	4.5
Others	3.2

Table 6. Methods of Selection

Recruitment and selection were seen to be major issues for Hong Kong operations in the PRC. The 1997 interviews confirmed that FIEs preferred to "recruit young people who have received modernized education... have a more open mind or have worked for foreign companies... if the person's abilitites do not match the foreign environment s/he must have special skills or good outside connections". In particular, some researchers have noted a tendency for FIEs to downplay the attainment of business degrees by Chinese applicants, unless these degrees involve some form of overseas experience or study (Bjorkman, et al., 1999).

It was seen by Hong Kong respondents to be important to recruit people who could match the company's culture. There were mixed views on the contribution of the former Foreign Enterprise Service Company (FESCO), one view being that it was an expensive "file-keeper", and the other that it performed a useful screening function. In fact, FESCO was a complex organisation, offering such supporting activities as benefits-management, allocation of staff, liaison with state agencies and other government organizations. Before 1992, Nicholson International (1999), as the China representative for Norman Broadbent International, reports that FESCO was the major recruiting agency. Since then, many of the world's top executive recruitment firms have set up China offices.

One FIE considered recruitment fairs very effective and there was evidence of information sharing amongst some FIE subsidiaries about recruitment methods and strategies. There was a great contrast in the recruitment options open to FIEs in terms of whether the operation was provincial, with a less educated and skilled labor market or in the more developed areas. In the first case often whole groups of people would be recruited and a great deal of sensitivity was needed to follow through a recruitment exercise. This would be more severe where the FIE was working on home country expectations.

PRC-based FIE responses were very similar to those based in Hong Kong. The following composite quotation gives some idea of the responses to this issue.

We recruit 50-60 graduates per year/ we interview twice (dept then HR), Dept head or above General Manager and assistant General Manager are involved/ we use internal recruitment and promotion works well and makes good use of HR staff/develops a recruitment plan based on the production plan. Sources are: students (they are paid for to have training), people with qualifications, labourers in ample supply hired on a contract basis, engineers - university graduates and experts from industry - 20-30 annually/ we only use university graduates as sales people Every employee has a 3 year contract.

There was no evidence that the recruitment and selection methods depicted in tables 5 and 6 had changed to any great extent. The same problems were mentioned and there was the same emphasis on the more technical and physical attributes of recruitees relative to the psychological testing which is more prevalent in the West. There was no mention of efforts to develop culturally correct tests although this is not to say that efforts had not been made.

Retention

A related issue to selection and recruitment is that of the retention of the recruited employee. To a much greater extent than would be expected in the Western setting the problem of retention was an all-consuming one in China. This can be predicted to remain an issue for many years to come, given the relatively low levels of educational development and the relatively high educational levels needed for China to realize its science and technology development as a way to enhance the economy. Respondents in the 1996 study grouped retention within the top three problems facing them (table 7).

Issues	Percentage
1. Quality of Management	10.9
2. Need for training and staff development/ development of training policy	8.6
3. High staff turnover/retention problem	8.0
4. Recognition of HR in business/lack of corporate support	8.0
5. Lack of remuneration and benefits policy/system	5.7
6. Government policies/legislation changes	5.7
7. Difficulties in recruitment and selection	4.6
8. Productivity and quality of staff to be improved	4.6
9. Lack of skilful labor	4.6
10. Staff attitude/morale/team work	4.6

Table 7. Major Problems Facing Human Resource Professionals

Staff retention was not mentioned specifically as a challenge in 1997 Hong Kong interviews. However in the PRC-based FIEs, it was considered to be an area of concern in most cases. Although salary and prospects within a company were the two main attractive elements for staff retention, the impression was that people did not always consider them together, rather they looked at salary only. One reason for this was that people who were not 'middle class' did not see work in a long term way. At other levels "some middle class PRC have plans for career development and retention is possible".

There was reporting of "vying" and job hopping and the FIEs mostly took a positive view of the future in this regard. Those in provincial areas relied to some extent on the difficulty of moving for some people. Those in city areas or special regions combined retention methods such as judicious payment of bonuses, extra non-work benefits with employee education and/or encouraging employees to take a longer, more developmental view of their future. Unusually, there was one enterprise who recorded no unwanted turnover over the past 18 years. The achievement was said to be contributed by the open management style of the company and its policy on people development and the career path of staff.

Retention was particularly problematic when enterprises invested several years in the development of managers, sometimes sending them overseas to study management and product-related skills. Apart from tying managers contractually, there were no easy solutions to this problem. An observation here is that some of the investment in engendering staff loyalty has not been as so well developed as in the case below, gathered in Hong Kong recently.

Loyalty to employees and an engendering of mutual staff trust are an important part of the HR strategy. This is demonstrated by the company's avoidance of redundancy if at all possible, even in difficult economic times. Despite the loss of some business, the company intends to redeploy staff from this area of the business. This commitment to employees produces a degree of loyalty towards the company.

Discipline is also essential because many of the guidelines given staff are for junior employees, most of whom have a poor education background and are not sufficiently trained to act on initiative.

The corporate commitments are communicated to staff through a number of different means. Recruits attend an orientation session for their first few days with the company where they are informed of the commitments. The new employees sign a statement acknowledging that they understand the corporate commitments. To supplement this initial familiarisation, a circular is distributed annually and it must be signed by staff to signal their acknowledgement. The contents of all company training courses incorporate the message of the commitments document.

However whilst researching for our 1990 book on management cases in Hong Kong (Tang, 1990), the situation in Hong Kong at that time was very like much the current China situation. Employers called the syndrome "job hopping" and it seemed at the time that there were two connected reasons for this development. One was that dissent and problems were best solved by leaving rather than disputation (the curves of disputes and unplanned labour turnover were inversely correlated with what could be expected in the West). This was, many people told us, so that the ritual networking lunches and reunions could be preserved. Another reason was that commitment was given more to family and friends than impersonal employers, especially those who did not design around a family concept (Whiteley & Jordan, 1991).

There is not yet a systemic approach to retention – this is understandable as employees of 'talent' come to realize their own value to employers. Horror stories of people asking for pay rises up to four times the going rate or the reasonable increase were more common than uncommon. Employers indicated that they might not always be in a position to wait until talent became less scarce and more available because of the need to remain competitive within the quality standards they required. The suggestion was that organizations would either begin to invest comprehensively in loyalty and commitment, as in the case above, or they would do the opposite and train technically, adopting a fatalistic view of turnover.

To summarise, an effective recruitment and selection system includes a thorough overview of the organisation's present and future activities. If possible, recruitment should take into account personal qualities as well as skills, so that work relationships as well as tasks are built into the process. Selection needs to be conducted in relation to job specifications, based on job analysis, and some investigation first needs to be conducted to see whether jobs need to be restructured or redesigned to suit future needs. Objectivity needs to be achieved through trade and other tests or evidence of qualifications and this needs to be tempered by relational requirements. Those close to the job or role need to be involved in selecting and it is at this stage that valuable relational needs should be added to employee specifications. An effective recruitment and selection system needs to be transparent, standardized where appropriate, objective and capable of predictive validity but also mindful of the very special intersubjective needs of the social group in the workplace. In addition, the issue of retaining those employees selected and recruited by the organization is a growing problem in the PRC as organizations continue to fight for a small number of talented local workers.

Human Resource (Manpower) Planning

An aspect of human resource management related to selection, recruitment, and retention of staff, particularly in a turbulent labor market, is that of human resource or manpower planning. Human resource planning is a major activity for the enterprise. It is more than ascertaining that the right people are in the right place at the right time at the right price, although this is daunting enough in itself. It is about the future of the organization. Eventually, as an organization evolves through its human resource planning cycles people should not be so much placed as perching. If the development system and the potential-spotting arm of the performance appraisal system (discussed later) is working, then plans should be made to relocate, stretch, and reskill people so that they have agility, and to hire others in order to ensure a smooth transition of skills within the organization.

Human resource planning is the unofficial function for managing change in an organization. Planning for the present is not effective in today's environment because the present is so brief. An effective human resource planning system is working on two fronts. The first entails anticipation of the people needed to fulfil production and sales commitments. Within this planning shares the load with training and development, appraisal and reward systems in facilitating quality and/or technology/innovation. The second front entails planning for change. This means ensuring flexibility and adaptability, generating strategies, policies and plans to make sure the right mix of people and technology, knowledge and skills are available should the enterprise have to change focus or direction.

The importance of human resource planning can be seen by the changing characteristics of the pool of available workforce within China over the past 5-10 years. Goodall and Burgers (1998:50) suggest that, according to executive-search firm Korn/Ferry International, the need for local executives will increase 400 percent during the next decade. This dramatic surge in demand for skilled workers has been brought about by the proliferation of FIEs within China, but also the current trend towards localization by many FIEs – replacing expatriates with local staff where possible (Nicholson International 1999).

An important component of human resource planning is career planning. It is cheaper to develop people to have careers within an organisation than to be in a constant state of recruitment and orientation (although this needs to be balanced with the need to infuse 'new blood' or fresh thinking). Accompanying career planning must be the provision of benefits to encourage employees to stick around long enough to maintain the career structure – organizations such as FESCO are providing help in this regard helping FIEs link to state-supported benefits for employees.

In addition, the activities of career planning and human resource planning demonstrate the organization's values very clearly – this is one area where workers at all levels can read the signs. Where there are vertical and horizontal paths for promotion and development there is evidence of an investment in people as well as a commitment to people. Where there are no plans or progression is erratic and reactive, a signal is sent that job movement is designed to suit the organization rather than the worker.

Under the title of Manpower Planning and Resourcing, several key activities were described by organisations operating within the PRC region. A large number of companies had formal documentation and/or systems of job specifications, job evaluation, and manpower (human resource) planning. 90% of the companies kept written job descriptions and 80% had personnel specifications. 83% had job evaluation schemes and 81% carried out human planning.

A large number of companies reported that human resource planning was carried out. The most popular method was human resource needs based on projected sales or orders (Table 8). A substantial number of companies relied on simple methods such as maintaining the existing staff ratios and guess work. However, as noted earlier, trends towards localization as well as stronger competition from competing organizations are likely to reduce the effectiveness of such a method of human resource planning.

Analysed by size of company, significantly more large companies used a projected sales/orders method than small companies. Analysed by industry, more companies in the manufacturing sector used a work study method and a higher proportion of companies in conglomerates used a statistical modelling method.

Method	Percentage
Projected sales/orders	48.0
Maintenance of present staff ratios	36.6
Work study	33.3
Careful guess work	22.8
Statistical modelling	20.3
Others	8.9

Table. 8 Methods of Manpower (Human Resource) Planning

Manpower (HR) planning was especially considered to be a key activity where the FIE had plans to localize.

manpower planning and training is very important in the coming years in consideration of localisation in 5 to 7 years and management and organisational changes (for existing plants) and new plants/sales centres to be set up

There were various responses to this function from Hong Kong enterprises operating in the PRC.

The manpower planning in the PRC is much influenced by the business objective in the PRC. As [this] business in the PRC is not very profitable, no manpower planning will be exercised before a clear business development is confirmed.

Human resource planning was very much a function of the ability to recruit, retain and feel some confidence in the commitment of employees.

Succession plan is very much related to staff retention. For small operations, local PRC staff with 3 to 4 years of working experience have the perception that they should be and will be considered for promotion .

Although there was a sense of FIEs having a long term view, it seemed as though the supporting systems for human resource planning such as management development, training, and retention had not yet yielded the sort of stable workforce that would allow sophisticated human resource planning to succeed.

Given the probability of reciprocated commitment from employee to organization (evidenced through increased tenure) with the implementation of devices such as career planning, it is perhaps ironic that a recent survey of managers found dissatisfaction with present position to be a key factor related to job movement in young Chinese professionals (Goodall et al., 1998). Predictably, the survey also found that job satisfaction was related to turnover, however one of the top factors in determining this job satisfaction was a manager's promotion prospects. Such findings suggest that those organizations waiting for the employment situation to "settle down" before instituting career planning (or other devices aimed at retaining employees) are likely to be losing more ground the longer they wait.

From our own research, although during the interviews with PRC based FIEs there was an underlying concern with human resource planning, not too much detail was given. Those enterprises that had a strategic human resource management approach incorporated it into the other human resource activities, linking human resource planning with career development, appraisal and compensation. Others, like the one below, were not prepared to invest.

[HR planning] is only conducted at an ad hoc basis, eg, transfer a person to meet an imminent need rather than based on long term development/ not to over train the staff to avoid retention problem arising and the business in the PRC has not yet been profitable

A provocative thought is that if human resource management was considered to be a genuinely valued business function, then human resource planning arrangements would be made at the stage of organizational design. Not only would they be made but they would be communicated as they developed, phase by phase. This is not just a point of interest. Goodall et al. (1998) have found that where career planning has been undertaken by FIEs, career plans have often not been fully communicated to the Chinese managers in a way that is likely to influence their turnover intentions. It would make sense for those FIEs who really were intending to be part of China's future to develop culturally sensitive planning. This would include some involvement in the training of China's workforce. The case below illustrates some of these points.

Case Study - Who is manning the phones at China Phone?

China Phone Company is jointly invested by The China Communications Control Board and two German parties. The Chinese side holds 60% of stock whilst the German firms hold 32% and 8% respectively. There are 2000 employees employed by the Company. In the fifteen years since the Company was established, production has steadily increased and the Company has gained nationwide fame. The Company has successfully won a number of "Top Ten Foreign Investment Firms' awards in China. China Phone has recently moved into the P'u tung Area into a splendid and elegant building in a similar type of 'business park' to those commonly found in overseas enterprises.

As a consultant working in the area of human resource planning, you have recently been asked to assist in a manpower planning strategy for the Company. The long term goals of China Phone are to become the biggest factory in the tele-communications industry and to make great contributions to the tele-communications field. As part of this goal, China Phone recognises the need to plan for the future. As shares holdings are held in China, there is a great feeling of 'nationalism' in the Company and the Company wishes to aid the economy in the best way it can. Goods are produced in large quantities in order to lower prices and capture a greater share of the market. Since the beginning of Company operations, prices have decreased by about two-thirds. As a result of this other companies have also had to lower their prices and the fall in the price of goods has been very beneficial to the end consumers.

The short term goal of the Company is to focus upon production and sales. Localization of production has reached 64% at this factory. Sixteen million units have been produced so far. Only one type of product is made at present but plans are being made to diversify in the future. Previously, much emphasis was placed upon increasing the amount of goods produced, however it is now realised that production is the basis for greater sales but sales must be increased in order to gain a larger share of the market.

Much effort is also now placed upon the quality of the end product as poor quality products will lead to a loss of revenue. The labor cost is about 3% of the total Company income and the cost of raw materials is below 55% of production costs. A reduction in the cost of raw materials is needed and it has become the task of the Purchasing department to seek out cheaper sources.

The Company is relatively weak in technological innovation. A research department has been established and about one-fifth of the workforce (three hundred people) are involved in research. The researchers are developing new products in order that the Company may put its diversification plans into action. Technology is basically transferred from the German partners – this is very clearly stated in the contract. The Chinese side now realise that they cannot rely solely upon their foreign partners and are interested in setting up a technical team.

It is believed at the Company that prices, quality and new products should be looked at as a whole. Lowering the prices is a strategy to gain a larger share of the market, prices have not been lowered because the goods are second-rate in any way, China Phone Company actually has a very good reputation in the market. There is, however, always room for improvement in quality and aftersales service. Business will also be improved when new products are developed.

The business strategy is determined by the Board of Directors who control a strategy team made up of the General Manager and his staff. The team puts forward strategic suggestions and carries out the plans finalized by the Board. The Department heads are responsible for strategic implementation and therefore understand the strategy, however it is felt that the general workers, who have little strategic knowledge, lack initiative. However from time to time, the General Manager holds meetings at which problems concerning the implementation of strategy discussed.

In talking with the Personnel Manager about the role of the HR department, you find out that he regards the HR department as one which should serve other departments and should therefore be able to work closely with them. For example, the Sales Department required a group of staff who were knowledgeable about the Company's products to work in ten new outlets and the Human Resources Department was responsible for their recruitment. The newly created positions were considered to be very challenging and many employees applied for the jobs. The Human Resources and Sales Departments had to work in close co-ordination with each other in order to recruit staff who met the criteria set by the Sales Department. The Personnel Manager informs you that currently, when a vacancy arises; the Department concerned will put forward names of people to be considered to fill the vacant post and the Human Resources Department will carry out the recruitment.

Generally speaking the staff turnover rate is low, in 1998 it was less than three per cent. Those who have been employed for under five years are more likely to leave than those who have worked in the factory for five years or more. Skilled workers who show good performance are given pay rises.

The main human resources strategy concerns the allocation of staff. Many posts are filled by internal recruitment and promotion, since this system works well at China Phone and makes good use of the Human Resources Department. As well as saving the Company the expense of recruiting from outside, it also gives employees greater incentive to work hard. All employees consider that salaries are the most important aspect of their jobs and training the second. Technical workers demand training and information about new innovations but those on the assembly line do not.

China Phone and its German parent companies have different methods of human resources management. The parent companies have been in operation for more than a century and have a more comprehensive approach but they are not efficient because of their adherence to a strict hierarchical order. The foreign staff are highly qualified but they are not willing to work overtime. However the hardworking nature of the local staff is highly praised by the German partners. The average production rate by local workers is three times that of foreign staff. Nevertheless new labor laws discourage overtime and there is the perception that this may result negative consequences for the Company.

Although all workers are basically treated equally, more leniency is shown towards the technical workers. For example, a plan is being made to allow them to have flexible working hours. A much stricter approach is taken when dealing with the general workers.

In discussing human resource planning with members of the Human Resource Department, they tell you that they feel better qualified individuals are needed. Young people generally want to get more for working less and many of them are irresponsible and feel that their jobs are a waste of time. There does not seem to be a solution to this problem; since internal promotion and transfer alone are not enough to meet the demands of such young people who need more guidance. If young people do not want to advance and build up careers the Company will not have a future.

Q1. What do you see as some of the manpower priorities in the next ten years in terms of new jobs and relevant skill sets at China Phone?

Q2. What are likely to be the likely impediments to any system of manpower planning at China Phone?

Q3. What cultural considerations need to be taken into account in providing a solution to these impediments?

Q4. In view of the need for more qualified staff, what are the options for China Phone in the recruitment and retention of employees?

Performance Appraisal

In designing effective career plans, and in ensuring that the right employees are promoted for the right reasons, some form of performance appraisal system is appropriate. An effective performance system is characterized as being multi purpose, multi method, of long-term orientation, with assessment criteria that cater for the future as well as the present. The purposes described by respondents in the 1996 study were ones associated with effective systems. These included: to assess past performance (often linked to pay); to set performance objectives; to assess training and development needs; to identify future potential, and to assist people in their career planning decisions.

Appropriateness is the key word in appraisal. Like other strategic human resource   functions, performance appraisal is linked to reward and training/development.

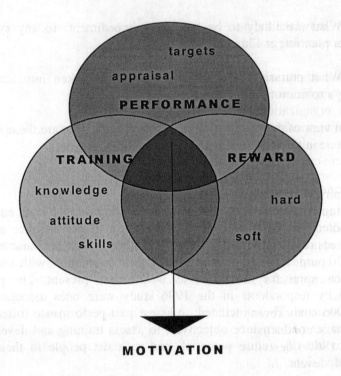

Figure 2. Performance, Training, Reward

Recognition needs to be made that there are many components contributing to, and detracting from, a person's performance (materials, supervision, training, social issues, other obstacles). Intrinsic to appraisal are the setting of goals or targets – these need to be constantly reviewed to be in line with changing or developing business strategies. The more these are agreed upon and owned by the worker or work group, the more likely commitment will be gained. Monitoring is to some extent a cultural issue. In some cultures monitoring is systematic and formal. In others it is more fluid and informal. For this reason appraisal systems are not normally transportable across cultures.

Standardization is important is cultures where fairness and accountability are issues and in such cases the appraisal systems must fulfil the cultural requirements of being objective, valid, reliable and above all, transparent.

Correctness may take the place of standardization where propriety and social conformance are integrated into performance.

Effective appraisal systems motivate, encourage continuous learning, produce an environment where mistakes are not hidden, and help people to internalize organizational goals and to keep on developing. On this basis the methods of appraisal are important. Simply cataloguing results is passive – combining results with coaching, mentoring and the ratee's ideas for improvement can be more productive.

In countries where equity is important this needs to be reflected in the system. In cultures like the Chinese setting, where there are areas of form and procedure, then these need to be catered for. Because of different cultural needs, total compensation systems are not normally transportable and they should be directly linked to the values incorporated in the performance appraisal system.

The 1996 study revealed some interesting data about how performance appraisal was conducted in FIEs. A large proportion of the responding companies (86%) described established systems of performance appraisal. Across all levels of staff, a results-oriented appraisal system and competency-based rating were the most popular methods used. For managerial/profession level, written reports and self-rating were most common.

Analysed by industrial sector, management by objective [MBO] for manual/technical levels was more prevalent in manufacturing than other sectors. Companies in industries other than manufacturing and conglomerates were more likely to use an alphabetical numerical rating for clerical/supervisory levels and written reports for managerial/professional grades (see table 9).

Method	Level	Percentage		
		Manual/ Technical	Clerical/ Supervisory	Managerial/ Professional
Results oriented/MBO		55.3	59.6	72.3
Alphabetical/numerical rating		24.1	29.1	15.6
Written report		21.3	38.3	47.5
Personality trait rating		14.2	21.3	17.7
Self-rating		18.4	31.9	42.6
Competency-based rating		33.3	41.1	48.2
Others		2.1	2.1	1.4

Table 9. Methods of Appraisal

Most companies had multiple objectives for implementing performance appraisals. The most popular reasons for appraising all levels of employees were to assess past performance, help improve current performance and set performance objectives (Table 10). Analysed by size, assessing past performance for manual/technician grades was more commonly quoted by small companies as the reason for having an appraisal system.

Purpose	Percentage		
	Manual/ Technical	Clerical/ Supervisory	Managerial/ Professional
To set performance objectives	50.7	60.9	79.7
To assess past performance	63.8	68.1	63.8
To help improve current performance	61.6	68.8	63.8
To assess training & development needs	44.9	55.8	52.2

To assess increases of new levels of salary	55.1	58.7	58.0
To assess future potential	42.8	58.7	59.4
To assist career planning decisions	24.6	46.4	43.5

Table 10.   Purposes of Appraisal

Analysed by industry, the common objectives for appraisal in industries other than manufacturing and conglomerates were using appraisals to assess past performance, help improve current performance and to assess training and development needs. Using appraisals for assessing the future potential of all levels of staff was also more prevalent in industries other than manufacturing and conglomerates. For clerical/supervisory staff, using the system to assist career planning decisions was prevalent in industries other than manufacturing and conglomerates. Analysed by nationality of ownership, US-owned companies were more likely to use appraisal results to assess training and development needs and to assess increases of new levels of salary for managerial/professional grades than were PRC-owned companies.

We attempted in the 1997 study to find out more about performance appraisal practices and we found some interesting similarities and differences in the qualtitative and qualitative data. Although the 1996 survey was supported in some areas of performance appraisal, in others it was clear that a less sophisticated situation was evolving.

In general, the trend was that the PRC management was following the Western style. The appraisal form used in the PRC was basically the one used worldwide although it was a Chinese-translated and simplified version. The results were not satisfactory as there could be 2 to 3 times of appraisal per year in order to get the approval for pay increment (3 times per year).

Due to the cultural difference, performance appraisal conducted in the PRC should be different... The company is just trying to set up a appraisal system in such a way the staff will grow and become the staff the company want them to be. Now the *company is just using a very primitive approach... Staff are involved in staff appraisal by saying what they think and what they feel before setting a target with their manager for their personal goal. The results of the appraisal system are linked up with the compensation system (which has been greatly modified for such purpose) to encourage them to meet the goal... Chinese employees do not focus on career development ($+ insurance) therefore simplified appraisal methods are needed for the PRC employees... Just one-page simplified performance appraisal form, having 6 to 7 assessing criteria is better.*

There were some comprehensive systems however – the two below were distinctive in that they were based on a concept to be understood and embraced.

The company has introduced and enforced a performance appraisal system. Initially, PRC people simply did not mentally accept it and during the assessment session, the score given to them was the only thing that mattered. With a 5-point measurement scale, if a 2-point was given to them,, they would only be disappointed. There is no alternative and the company had to educate them to understand and accept the concept and demonstrate the company's belief in performance appraisal through training courses; and make sure that performance appraisal is an on-going process. The management is requested not to do performance appraisal just for the sake of appraisal. There should be coaching, performance feedback and discussions throughout the year...

There is a performance management system which is objective, goal oriented, and which includes i) the target (eg. sales volume) to be met and whether a target is acceptable to top management will depend on whether it is feasible and does not fall behind the market; ii) the staff's technical knowledge; iii) customer services (ability to retain and attract customers), and iv) ability in problem solving and influencing people. Performance of staff is checked throughout the year.

A two-way approach is adopted for evaluation (mutual responsibility): If a staff cannot meet the goal, there will be evaluation to see if there is sufficient guidance, coaching and training provided by the supervisor/ the company to the staff, or if the staff fits into the corporate culture. In the second case, some creative methods, e.g. job rotation, have to be made or we may have to terminate the employment relationship on an acceptable basis. The staff are educated to understand and accept the concept of the system and the clue is that "provided you are upfront and constructive, most people can accept criticism."

Although Bjorkman et al. (1999) comment that "of all HR management practices covered in our study, performance appraisal was most similar to companies' global policies as they implement their global performance appraisal systems in their Chinese organizations" (Bjorkman et al., 1999: 19), problems were reported in adopting contemporary methods such as the 360° method where subordinates become 'assessors', reporting on their supervisors and managers. "The 360% method has not been introduced in the PRC as the PRC nationals are not mature enough and because local PRC [people] are very resentful at the idea of being assessed by subordinates".

This promoted the need for human resource managers to carry out review meetings, to complement appraisal by varied communication methods such as staff newsletters, briefings by supervisors, and to include appraisal as part of leadership training. The 1997 interviews supported the 1996 findings that comprehensive and career development appraisal would be more prevalent in hi-tech and service industries than in manufacuring and even some service industries in the PRC.

Some PRC-based interviews differed from those in Hong Kong in two ways. First there was a more varied response, ranging from reports of very simple evaluation to more holistic and integrated systems:

Managers use the Company's Performance Management System to communicate with their staff. It is also used as a tool for training up managers. Managers will talk to and evaluate their staff on a quarterly basis. Four steps are involved: At the beginning of a year, goals are set and both sides commit to achieving them. Report of progress is September. Evaluation is December. The Company's HR Department emphasises fairness to all employees.   More skill is required from employees at the management level and different evaluation items are involved during performance assessment.   Compared to general staff, employees at the manager level are evaluated on one additional item – management skill – during assessment.

[we] evaluate our staff through a goal achievement evaluation system. Standards are set every three months. Each employee is evaluated through a points system. Points directly affect salary and promotion promotion is for 60% general employees Also has job rotation scheme

Second, performance appraisal was not always recognized as a motivational or diagnostic device. At one end of the FIE spectrum, personnel were hired, fired and replaced in a simple way. This was possible in a buyer's market and there was usually no commitment to the worker. Inspection of work in this instance was the nearest thing to appraisal. At the other end there was a mix of appraisal purposes and methods. An intrinsic weakness in appraisal systems, not only in Hong Kong and the PRC was also the training of raters. This also seemed to be the case in the PRC. The fact that no mention was made of difficulties in this area of training may indicate that it is not well recognized as problematic. However, in a survey conducted by Bjorkman et al. (1999), numerical performance ratings were shown to be used less for direct appraisal of past performance, and rather, in a less threatening manner, for example, for future training and development.

Considering appraisal was taking place with Chinese people there were few examples of informal appraisal, team appraisal or other creative, perhaps 'soft' methods. As things stood, the indication was that, on the surface at least, Western appraisals would be put in place and it was only a case of waiting until Chinese workers could learn to understand them. What may go on beneath the surface, of course, as many Hong Kong employers and employees have told us, is likely to be a second unseen system where the workers use their own 'face-sensitive' methods to motivate and improve performance. In a 'two-system' scenario, not only is energy wasted and activities duplicated but one of the systems, the informal one, is likely to be controlled in a way that might not always match the organizational culture. This is an important point, since even where performance appraisal systems are implemented in line with Chinese values, the organizational culture may still prove a powerful influence on the effectiveness of the system. Such an influence is evident in the case study below.

Case Study - Making a Point at the Shanghai Partner Store

A colleague has recently approached you to work on a performance evaluation system with Shanghai Partner Store Co. Ltd. a company situated in Hung Ch'iao, an area in which banks, commercial buildings and hotels cluster. The company is a joint venture company with 65% of investment from Shanghai and 35% from Hong Kong. The Company employs just over 700 employees.

The performance appraisal system used at Partner Stores is somewhat unique. Each employee has a points record book. If the employee breaks a rule, points are deducted. Points are added when there is an accomplishment. The Personnel Department is responsible for keeping and managing a record of these points.

The Personnel Department evaluates each department head using the point system. The results are given to the General Manager to review and are kept as a part of the performance evaluation.

The Company uses a four star performance method every year for the middle level managers. Before the end of each year, these middle level managers are required to write a paper on management. The General Manager and the Assistant General Managers form a debate committee, in which each department head has to defend his position in-front of the committee and is subject to evaluation by points.

Comments from employees and managers alike have indicated that this system is not too effective in providing feedback, giving incentives for good performance, and optimizing progress towards the Company's strategic goals. The Company uses the same system to evaluate every year, however it is felt that an easy-to-use and effective evaluation system needs to be developed.

The Company's strategy is to build up a good reputation, to establish business direction, to maintain a systematic work flow and to provide values. The business slogan is "to establish the Company in this small community, then move onto something greater." The short term goal of the Company is to achieve a sales revenue of 5 billion dollars in 2000. To achieve the company's strategy and the short-term goal, the General Manager believes that the Company needs to work on the following 3 areas:

- i)   Increasing training. The three year old work force is the backbone of the Company, and it needs to be retained.
- ii) Adjusting product range. There is a need to attract both the high income residents and the low income residents in the small district.
- iii) Emphasizing sales. The Company holds various community chest activities to pay back the community.

The Company is also concerned about cost reduction. since price competition is one of the major focuses in a competitive market and cost reduction provides for low prices which attract customers. Improving the quality of service is also a priority. Most of the Partner stores have similar product pricing, so good service also attracts regular customers and increase sales. Each counter salesperson is required to have knowledge of the quality of the product, its nature and its usage, as well as being able to understand the customers' needs.

The Personnel Department is busy in managing personnel matters and is not therefore involved in formulating Company strategy. The most important human resource strategy is training and development. The training program is designed in accordance with the need of the industry.

The Partner Stores serve mainly foreign tourists. The sales staff are therefore required to speak good English and Japanese. They also need to have professional knowledge in areas such as antiques, cultural arts and home appliances. This requires training.

As with many enterprises in China, the Company is very concerned about the stability of the work force. It is hoped that the performance evaluation system can also aid in alleviating some of this concern. In order to stabilize the work force, especially the high proportion of "Chih Ts'ing" (educated young people), the Company would like to launch a series of initiatives. The performance evaluation system is seen as a further opportunity to stabilise the workforce.

Q1. Why might the form of evaluation described be ineffective for this company?

Q2. What might the company do to improve the evaluation process and to stabilise the workforce?

Q3. What other HR processes might be used to alleviate some of the concerns of management and to achieve some of the Company's goals?

Compensation, remuneration and benefits

In relation to FIEs, Swaak (1995) presents some examples of the ways compensation packages may differ according to the structure of the enterprise, and makes the point that different forms of FIEs may require different activities from the human resource manager:

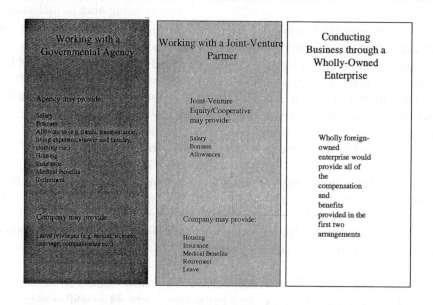

Figure 3. Some different forms of Foreign Invested Enterprise

Adapted from Swaak, 1995: page 45)

An effective compensation system takes the opportunity of rewarding in as many ways as possible. This is in contrast to an efficient compensation system which takes the opportunity of rewarding on a calculative basis - either pay for hours worked or pay for pieces of work completed. Additional to what the respondents term the 'dollars and cents' scenario, there are some important things that money can not buy, things that are important to the enterprise. These are valued differently in each case, depending on the vision and mission of the organization as well as the way in which this is communicated and agreed upon by employees. Non-tangible benefits would characteristically include trust, honesty, loyalty, respect and commitment. However, once again there is an etic and emic aspect to these values. In the West, an individual would be the likely target of personal trust and respect, with personal and individual qualities being the ones gaining or losing respect. In the Chinese setting there may well be the same titles, such as trust, however the expressions and targets of them might be very different.

A comprehensive reward system would include values as part of rewards, first investigating what they might be for different groups of worker. In our study of IT professionals, we found that not feeling valued far outstripped rewards such as enhanced software and better hardware. When compensation is viewed in a wider context, management skills (soft rewards) and actual pay and benefits (hard rewards) overlap. It is soft or tacit information related to meaningful rewards that managers need to be able to access. To do this they need to be able to come close to the workforce.

In the 1996 study, pay for employees of over 70% of the responding companies was unilaterally determined by management (Table 11). Negotiations with trade unions or staff associations were rarely used by small companies. Individual negotiations with employees were less common in companies in the manufacturing sector.

Wages and salaries were usually reviewed annually (table 12). However, a number of companies carried out a pay review every six month's especially for the manual/technician and clerical/supervisory levels. This is particularly seen as an important strategy when one considers the previous notes of salary being a top factor for retention of staff. As noted by Bjorkman et al. (1999), some organizations in China have established policies which commit them to remain in the top 25% in terms of salary levels.

| | Level | Percentage | | |
Method		Manual/ Technical	Clerical/ Supervisory	Managerial/ Professional
Individual negotiations with employees		17.6	20.3	25.0
Unilateral decision by management		70.3	76.4	75.0
Negotiations with trade union/staff association		20.3	16.9	17.6

Table 11. Method of Determining Pay

| Grade | Percentage | | | |
	Every 6 months	1 year	2 years	Other
Manual/Technical	13.8	73.0	3.3	6.6
Clerical/Supervisory	10.5	78.3	3.3	5.9
Managerial/Professional	9.2	77.0	4.6	6.6

Table 12.   Wage and Salary Review

Many responding companies (90.8%) had an incentive scheme. The most popular type of incentive scheme was discretionary bonus, followed by individual Payment By Results [PBR] (Table 13). Small companies used group PBR more often than large companies for manual/technician grades and clerical/supervisory grades. The use of discretionary bonuses as incentive payment for clerical/supervisory grades was found to be more popular in small companies.

Grade	Percentage				
	Individual PBR*	Group PBR*	Commission	Profit Sharing	Discretionary Bonus
Manual/Technician	51.1	25.2	5.2	9.6	71.1
Clerical/ Supervisory	51.1	22.2	8.9	9.6	73.3
Managerial/ Professional	53.3	23.7	9.6	14.8	74.1

Table 13. Incentive Scheme

70.2% of the responding companies reported that they had a retirement scheme whilst a pension scheme was most common amongst these companies. Of those companies that did not have such a scheme, 55.3% said that they planned to introduce one (Table 14).

Type	Percentage
Provident scheme	24.8
Pension scheme	70.4
Final salary scheme	4.8
Others	5.6

Table 14. Retirement Scheme

From responses of Hong Kong enterprises operating in the PRC, it was obvious that wide wage relativities between low value and high value workers were prevalent in the PRC environment. The sentiment below was strongly reflected in other PRC cases.

development and marketing (which were mainly in HK) were regarded as highest value skills, and the value of skills (manufacturing) in the PRC was lowest ranked, compared to HK and other regions; and thus the focus of manufacturing was to lower the cost.

Bearing the above in mind, the specter of wages drift was reported by almost all interviewees. The following quotations give some idea of the forces at work.

First there is the problem of expectations. According to a survey conducted in the PRC by a survey company, a very high percentage of the fresh graduates expected to earn RMB 5,000 to RMB 6,000 monthly, but the actual average was around RMB 2,000.

There was also the preoccupation of 'dollar and cents' (linked to the difficulties of persuading staff to take a career perspective of their future). It seemed that at this stage in the development of PRC workers, the dollar was a chief motivator.

"Dollar and Cents" was the major reason for employee turnover. This was especially the case for those young and freshly educated, they always wanted to earn a very high salary.

There was a view that "the dollar will diminish as a motivator as the PRC becomes more prosperous". However, in the meantime there was an understandable reluctance to invest too much in unskilled groups relative to skilled workers. With skilled workers there was often a "pay needs to be linked to performance and years of service" approach. The notion of providing "reasonable accommodation, food, and other utilities to workers who come from other provinces (mainly from the country side such as Guangdong)" was common as was the provision of other 'buffers' that used to be provided by the state, such as a retirement scheme.

If PRC nationals change from poverty to middle class, monetary-incentive is very useful for staff motivation and this is the tactic in early years in PRC to hunt people in the market. And now the economy is more prosperous, and PRC nationals are just changing from middle class to upper middle class, the marginal effect of the dollar certainly diminishes. The company integrates performance, pay and staff development in such a way that the remuneration package is related to staff performance and years of service

In particular, it was noted that the situation in the PRC regarding compensation is quite complex, especially where there is a Chinese partner. "Regarding the flexibility in pay, joint ventures have the least flexibility as the PRC partners have a say and there is no particular regional difference. For representative offices, officially salary is not flexible but actually it will all depend on the situation". Local enterprises were not seen to be too much of a problem.

FIEs can provide better cash salary (2 to 3 times of the latter) and faster track promotion. This is particularly crucial to the people who work in fast developing cities, e.g. Shanghai, where inflation is serious.

The basic salary provided by PRC local enterprises is normally very low. Nevertheless, PRC local enterprises traditionally also provide other benefits to staff: eg, accommodation, and various types of subsidies. the enterprises are now cutting these benefits and improving salary but there is still a gap compared to foreign companies. Accommodation is very important to local PRCs. However, many national enterprises have poor management and most of them may have to face bankruptcy, and thus providing accommodation to staff is a tremendous burden to them. Therefore, if staff are already living in the apartments provided by the enterprise, they are advised to buy the accommodation themselves. If staff have yet been provided apartments, then they will never be accommodated.

There was also an indication that an integrated approach with other processes (such as training) was preferred, but this was not always feasible, often because of the 'dollars and cents' issue.

We are trying to integrate the 3 elements, ie, performance, pay and training, with an implementation of a mechanism (performance management system) over various operations including Hong Kong, the PRC and other places. The system is linked with the pay increase, and it is called the "positive reinforcement cycle".

The overall problem in the PRC seemed to be market competition, especially for 'young talent' and skilled labor. In keeping with this it was not always possible to acquire accurate labor market intelligence in terms of the going rate for different jobs. At the same time the topic of wages was subject to rumor and expectations were many times the sensible rate for the job.

the company uses low labor costs to decrease production costs and increase market share - although has to offer 15% annual pay rise to motivate staff Also bonuses are given salary itself is based on academic qualifications

Those who work for the Company not only enjoy a competitive compensation package but also work in a safe and comfortable environment and enjoy many other benefits including unemployment and medical insurance, pension funds and housing allowances. All of these things help to provide stability and security to the lives of the employees and thus improve their standards of work. It is believed that it is important to provide for material needs as it ties the personal needs of the staff to the needs of the Company.

The main human resource focus is on salary and benefits. The Company believes that higher salaries are the main reason that people wish to work for a Company with foreign investors. Overall, the workers here are better paid than other local workers in the same industry.

Salary is low and the employees still stay - the reason for staying is close location and there is a recession from state enterprises which makes unemployment high and therefore staff more available.

On top of basic salaries a holistic approach is taken where attention is paid to whether or not the jobs are challenging. Department heads are taught to be considerate to the needs of the workers. Jobs are rotated amongst employees.

Even though there was recognition of China as a growing economy, old in some ways and young in others, there was a sentiment that if things continued to develop in the same way, the competitive edge of labor cost would quickly be lost. The quotations above give a sense of the very different outlooks held by PRC-based FIEs concerning reward systems. Nevertheless there was a theme running through the interviews of nervousness at what unrealistic expectations could do to profitability and sustainability, a theme noted in the final case study of this chapter.

Case Study - The Price of Progress at Fast Food Corporation

FFC Burger is a renowned fast food production and retail company with over 20,000 retail stores worldwide. It has been expanding its business in an astonishing fashion during recent years. There are currently 235 restaurants operating in 41 Chinese cities. The majority of these restaurants are located in the south and east of China.

The Company has been having some problems with attracting and retaining its Beijing staff. The Vice President of the Company has recently invited you to assist in the development of a salary package for the Company's employees in Beijing in order to motivate them to further achieve the Company's aims and in order to show the Company as an attractive employment prospect for prospective employees.

The Vice President tells you that all FFC Burger stores in Beijing are managed by the Beijing FFC Burger Company Limited - a joint venture between the China Textile Corporation and the FFC Burger Corporation, U.S. This arrangement is unlike other joint ventures of FFC in China where the US Corporation is the sole or major stock holder. In this case, Beijing FFC Burger Company Limited is equally owned by the two companies and therefore, has a good deal of autonomy in the structuring of its compensation and benefits packages.

You note that FFC has a number of short-term business goals:

- Achieving 100% customer satisfaction
- Expanding market share
- Low price, good value through managing cost to reduce the need for price increases (notwithstanding inflation).

The ultimate aim is to gain regular customers. The Company lets customer needs guide its long-term investment. This is believed to be the way for continuous long-term business development.

An important long-term goal for FFC is localization of both labor and materials. There are currently 400 full-time employees and 600 part-time employees within the Company. The HR Department acts as a consultant to help each department head to manage their employees and does not directly manage the productivity of staff. HR managers are trained on the job. However recruitment and training cannot keep pace with the rapid business development and expansion of the Company. This is despite the large number of training specialists who are constantly employed to conduct training programs for employees of the Company.

Regarding recruitment, it is the HR Department's responsibility to recruit high quality employees according to requirements set out by various departments. Applicants are interviewed twice, first by the respective department and next by HR Department. When recruiting staff for the position of department head or above, the General Manager and Assistant General Manager are involved in the process and make selection decisions. The HR Department in particular recognizes that a powerful incentive for recruitment would be the new salary package.

Until recently, the Company has not been overly concerned about labor turnover, since high employee mobility is one of the major characteristics found in FFC. The Human Resource Department focuses particularly on the retention of high quality and high performance employees. Here again, appropriate benefits and compensation schemes are seen to be extremely important. The HR Department makes long term development of employees their main responsibility; they spend only 10% of their time in other daily operations such as preparing salary slips. In addition, the in-house promotion rate has reached 65% for general employees – this is an accomplishment that other companies can only dream of. A job rotation scheme also brings variety and interest into employees' work.

Currently salary is based on performance and is considered as part of the whole compensation package. In the past, this arrangement has avoided an adverse effect on salary level due to minor changes in the market, however FFC is now facing pressure from the upward trend in management salaries (particularly in Beijing) and is keen to retain its impressive track record of retention of staff. In particular, the Human Resource Department is involved in the drawing up of the Company's strategic plan and sees its ability to plan for the future strongly tied to its ability to recruit and retain the best-qualified employees. When considering the make-up of the Employee Compensation Plan, the Department understands it will need to consider many factors, such as types of employees required, organization development, and operation effectiveness.

Q1. The activities of the Human Resource Department at FFC indicate possible use of a wide range of compensation mechanisms in order to attract and retain employees. Given the goal of localization, what sorts of compensation are likely to work best for the Chinese employees?

Q2. How would these forms of compensation be best utilised in practice in order to attract and retain employees – are there any particular key stages of the recruitment or employment process at which a package may be best implemented?

Q3. How could you best make the package applicable to the short and long-term goals of FFC?

6.   The Greatest Directness is Flexible - Compatible Paradigms

Compatible Paradigms : Complex Adaptive Systems and Chinese Relational Systems

We have spent years moving pieces around, building elaborate models, contemplating more variables, and creating more advanced forms of analysis. Until recently we really believed that we could study the parts, no matter how many of them there were, to arrive at knowledge of the whole. We have reduced and described and separated things into cause and effect and drawn the world in lines and boxes. (Wheatley, 1994:27)

Earlier in the book we talked about the Western paradigm for doing business. We suggested that over the years, the philosophy and methodologies developed into an orthodoxy. We pointed out that in the past thirty years, many edifice changes were made. These were changes that appeared to be radical but which, by utilizing orthodox language and frameworks, did not alter the foundations upon which Western business was built. Some of these changes included the move in business and human resource methodologies from increased to decreased control, and from decreased to increased autonomy. An emphasis on the processual, and, in the strategic planning area, less extrapolation and more imaginal activities has characterized changes in competitive organizations.

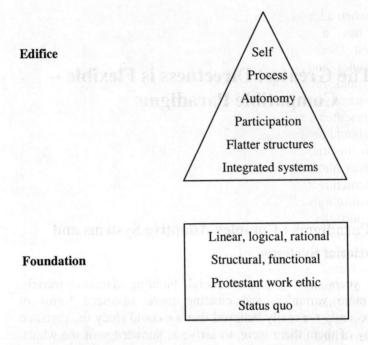

Figure 1. The edifice and underlying foundation

The human being (employee) began to come into focus as more than an extension of a machine and/or a manager's mind.

The results of many of these changes have been embodied in the modern (and modernist) conception of human resource management. The flagship human resource management organizations can be noted for their emphasis on the personal self development of their managers and employees. In many cases, vertical integration is to be found in the guise of special project teams and a matrix design. Included in the key performance indicators of managers and especially senior managers would be a capability for interdepartmental relations. Terms like "multiple career paths" give a hint of one of the most prominent features of modern business. This is their integrated linear, sequential and externally organized nature. If we look at these concepts, we can gain some insight into the Western business psyche.

Integration, when adopted in such a way as to preserve the character of each element has a particular quality. This is the quality of institutionalization (Scott, 1987). Institutionalization occurs when key organizing principles and key activities (social, functional, educational, legal, economic and relational) are designed around a theory of the organization (or society). The assumption is that these are accepted in the form they are presented (usually by those in power) as though everyone agreed that they should be this way. Once the activities are solidly followed, they develop into 'institutions'. Eventually, the collection of these become known as the status quo. Given a strong paradigm such as the structural-functional superstructure that has characterized Western society (Morgan 1980b), a set of institutions can very soon develop into an operational as well as overall status quo. Because everyone is thought to agree on the sort of organization (or society) depicted by the institutions, it becomes unnecessary to examine the underlying philosophies and assumptions. These are embodied in the formal system of rules, procedures, policies, and the informal system of rituals, ceremonies, stories and conversations. This happens to the extent that it is easy to get out of the habit of questioning and analyzing at a deep level. Questioning assumptions seriously would mean unraveling the intertwined threads of the interactions and interdependencies of the institutions. If the organization has existed for some decades, the interactions will have become sophisticated and intricate, almost impossible in some cases to separate.

This produces problems concerning change (such as the change required to embrace the sort of mindset to operate in harmony with Chinese ways). Rigidity is endemic in well-institutionalized organization. This begins with a structural inability to handle change. If the status quo becomes the bed rock for every facet of the organization, then to change it radically would cause organizational collapse. Some management writers have called such organizations autopoietic (Whiteley, 1999b).

> *Autopoietic systems display qualities of evolutionary invariance, self organization to perpetuate the system's status quo, self referential activities and attempts to organize aspects of the environment to suit the system's needs. Systemic characteristics include a desire to return to equilibrium and to be resistant to evolutionary change. (Whiteley, 1999b)*

Using the PATOP model (Whiteley, 1999c) we can begin to build a map of this first part of a developing model, using other workers as a focus.

	Modernism/Scientific Management
	Rational/economic being
Philosophy	Values efficiency
	Reward with money
Assumptions	Motivate with money
	Develop machines, systems
Theory	to enhance efficiency: linear thinking
	Worker as extension of
Organization	Machine/a recipient of orders
	Deskilling, specificity of
Practices	Tasks and roles, compliance and obedience

Figure 2. The Scientific Paradigm

Philosophically the true nature of the human at work within this paradigm is that s/he is rational economic in nature. The assumption is that therefore the person will want to be rewarded with the management system which provides the most money. The approach that matches this is a rational and impersonal approach, taking into account the machine-like rather than the creative aspects of the worker. In order to produce the most money, the work will need to be organized efficiently with disregard for social and personal tastes (and distractions) in doing the job. It has long been "known" from this perspective, that the most efficient way to design jobs is to take out variety and autonomy and to match worker skills with those useful for the single proven best way to do the job (see Emery [1993] for critical comment on this).

Robert Maxfield (1999) was a product of the standard systems approach to management. He co founded a company that grew to 10,000 people. He and his co founders used their linear systems approach to management.

> *Need to make a decision? Apply decision analysis; define all the possible consequences of all the possible actions one might take, then assign probabilities and value functions to these various outcomes, then compute expected values and ascertain the "optimal" decision. Worried about competition? Apply game theory. It did not take long to realize that this "engineering" approach was unsuitable for the rapidly changing environment which I was in. (Maxwell, 1999:2)*

He reflected, years after this experience when discovering complex adaptive systems theory, that there was a deeply embedded metaphor in our society that worked strongly against adaptable organizations – the metaphor of the organization as a machine. This is basically what is described above (except that not only the organization, but the worker, and to some extent, the management, also came to be praised for their machine-like qualities). Maxwell pointed out that we are all familiar with the end result of applying the machine metaphor. Organizations often have precisely defined organizational charts with many hierarchical levels, volumes of procedures defining most activities of the organization and major decisions vested in few central individuals who have ultimate authority.

It is very clear that the Western paradigm, fashioned as it was for a world of stability, relatively undereducated and unself-aware workers, long product runs and reasonably differentiated markets, is unsuitable for the future that business faces. Almost every characteristic is different. The world is becoming turbulent and stability (rather than turbulence) will be in pockets rather than the other way round. Dynamism is a word that comes to mind, as business sees itself as on the move, needing to embrace technological changes almost daily and in many cases needing multiple products or variations to cope with the increasingly undifferentiated and short run product lines. A characteristic of Western business methodologies was the collection of data to ensure the continuity of and compliance to institutional, procedural requirements. This took time that is now not available. An example of the unsuitability for some of these stable, institutionalized processes is modern performance appraisal. By the time conventional performance appraisal methods are used (i.e., targets set, monitoring arrangements put in place, data on performance collected, performance appraisal interviews held and the results fed back into overall organizational performance), the whole scenario for the business may have changed. With an emphasis on functional reviews and continuous (minor) refinements of processes and systems in this day and age, the world can pass by. It is becoming a serious issue in the West to find a paradigm for business that matches the characteristics of the complex, global dynamic environment. Paradigms such as the one below, predicated as they are on evolution, adaptation, and self organization offer one alternative and coincidentally, one that has the potential to harmonize with the adaptive and relational elements of Chinese business.

Complex Adaptive Systems

I no longer believe that organizations can be changed by imposing a model developed elsewhere...the new physics cogently explains that there is no objective reality out there waiting to reveal its secrets, there are no recipes, or formulae, no checklists or advice that describe 'reality'. There is only what we create through our engagement with others and events. (Wheatley 1994:151)

Such a paradigm has been evolving for several years now. Coming from groups like the Santa Fe Institute (which is populated by Nobel prize winners and some of the best brains in the US and Europe) is an emerging paradigm based on Complex Adaptive Systems (CAS) theory. Currently CAS is more in the form of a metaphor than a robust paradigmatic framework. It does, however, have characteristics much more harmonious with the Chinese culture than the modernist, scientific management engineering metaphor (Taylor 1929). Coming ironically also from the physical science discipline the metaphor is one of emergence, non linearity, co-evolution, self-organization and, above all, adaptiveness.

It is not easy to define Complex Adaptive Systems. One of the most effective ways to do this is to relate its characteristics. CAS is an open system, meaning that the system is open to the many variations that are incorporated as 'virtual realities' in the human's repertoire (Hayles, 1994). Variations come from the endless and continuous improvisations made by the human brain as it meets situations. The brain, the mood, the attitudes and beliefs of people superimpose upon each experience so that it becomes unique to that person. An open system, in CAS terms consists of many heterogeneous agents, that is, different sorts of people.

These people interact, not in a linear and sequential fashion but in response to things that emerge and trigger an action or interaction. An action in a complex adaptive system is decided upon as a response to the continuous adaptation to anticipated responses of other people. In some cases an action is co created as individuals survey their possible responses and out of these co create an action. (Kauffman, 1995). Complete knowledge and predictability of people is not attempted in the complex adaptive system. It is acknowledged that spontaneity replaces predictability and that an element of emergence will be present in any planned action. Even now, before we explore this area further, it is evident that CAS is more like some of the Chinese relational characteristics of fluid actions, adaptation to others as they are adapting in return, and a tolerance of ambiguity and variation in the responses of others.

Characteristics of CAS

According to Maxfield (1999) there are four major properties of CAS. These are: self-organization, evolutionary trajectories, co-evolution, and punctuated equilibrium.

Self-organization refers to the seeming tendency for systems to formulate new patterns of behavior and new entities, arising from responses to interactions with others (who are, and are often observed to be, interacting with others as well). A key feature of self organizing is nesting. An individual, (the lower level of CAS) interacts with others. These become a group, the next level up. The group becomes a system and interacts with other groups to produce new entities.

In the Chinese business setting the family system is very important. The individual interacts with others and they all belong to a family. Remember that in the Chinese culture, a family can include workmates and the family system is often preferred as a model for adaptive behaviors within organizations.

Evolutionary trajectories

This is a very important concept concerning the received wisdom of strategic and other long term planning. It means that the future is not considered as an extrapolation of the past. This is because it is seen to be constantly evolving. Knowing how things are in the present or in the past does not mean that a prediction is possible that could describe the future. As we see from some of the concepts in chaos theory (Gleick, 1996), minute disturbances in the initial conditions of a phenomenon can have disproportionate results, hence the butterfly effect, and the saying that a songbird flapping its wings in the Summer Palace can cause a storm in Hong Kong. Rather than predictability and precision, it is better to have resilience and flexibility. These will be difficult concepts to incorporate into Western mindsets but the environment may leave no choice but to seek new and more evolutionary ways to respond to the speed of change.

Co Evolution

Co evolution is the next generation in thinking from Darwin's natural selection theory of evolution. Co evolution does not take the rather stable view of the environment in which characteristics of the fittest are isolated. It is founded on the concept of a constantly changing landscape where fitness rests upon anticipation and adaptation. Interactions with people who are, in turn, adapting to the interactions of others and factoring these adaptations into their own interactions give a sense of the essentially dynamic and adaptive. Together, people are co evolving. Maxfield (1999) provides an example of how people co evolve with artifacts. As the abacus was replaced by the calculator, human activity had to adapt to the new ways of organizing the thinking. A further example could be the content in this book. If the ideas are accepted by Westerners and are adapted for use in the Chinese setting then co evolution will have occurred. As we reach the information age in earnest, we can anticipate many instances of co evolution as previously stable business activities such as distribution and warehousing, segmentation of markets, patterns of consumer buyer behavior and other key functional activities are affected by technology.

Punctuated Equilibrium

One of the biggest anecdotal comments about foreign business methodologies is the apparent certainty that things will remain stable, for example for the duration of a contract. This is accompanied by an attempt to predict the future so that any contingencies that might predictably arise are catered for contractually. The complaint is that this is a methodology that automatically assumes lack of trust, the inability of business partners to adapt to unforeseen circumstances and the assumption that equilibrium is the desired condition (Trompenaars, et al., 1998). This is, of course connected to the logical, rational, impersonal and certainty needs of the modernist mindset (Weisbord, 1987). As Stacey (1998) points out, these organizations have a need to organize so that they can always return to equilibrium, the status quo, to certainty and a belief that the systemic frameworks upon which they build the organization will not change. This concept is closer to the notion of unpunctuated equilibrium.

The notion of punctuated equilibrium is an acknowledgement that whilst there may be periods, even long periods of equilibrium, these can be punctuated at any time by bouts of very rapid change and disequilibrium. At these times, the notion of dissipative structures comes into play. The theory behind this concept is very well described by Prigogine (1996), Roeland (1991) Jantsch (1980) and other writers in the complexity theory field. Rather simplistically, dissipative structures occur in non equilibrium systems. Where there are non linear relationships combined with unexpected and unanticipated change, new organizational configurations are necessary. When the balanced system breaks down under these pressures, the system becomes open to the environment, importing energy and exporting entropy (or waste). As the unnecessary energy is dissipated, new structures emerge in a way that could not be predetermined. It has been predicted for some time that not only are these ideas feasible but that some Western organizations are embracing the concept and learning to live on what Brown and Eisenhardt (1998) call 'the edge of chaos'. This is where, according to several complexity theorists including Kauffman (1995), Stacey (1996), and Brown and Eisenhardt (1998), processes of adaptation will allow a change from predictable rules to generative rules, from linear causal thinking to non linear dynamical thinking.

Using these characteristics, we can contrast the PATOP content of modernist, scientific management with that of complex adaptive systems management. P is Philosophy (in this case the 'true nature' of the human at work) A is Assumptions (in this case about how such a person should be rewarded and motivated), T is the theory behind the organizing, O is the organizing itself, that is, the structures systems and processes that circumscribe the worker's environment and P is what they mean in practice at the workface level.

Again we will focus on the philosophical question about the nature of the human at work.

	Modernism/Scientific Management	Complex Adaptive Systems of Management
P	A rational/economic being	An adaptive, anticipatory and interactive being
A	Reward with money-making conditions	Reward with adaptation opportunities
	Calculative psychological Contract*	Collaborative psychological contract
T	Worker as extension of Machine/a recipient of orders	Worker as an adaptive organism, co creating solutions
O	Develop machines, systems To enhance efficiency: linear thinking	Design relational structures optimize feedback mechanisms
P	Deskilling, specificity of Tasks and roles, compliance and obedience	Mix of specificity and discretion Roles flexible and responsive to change

Figure 3. Traditional and New paradigms

Chinese Relational System

Chinese culture has manifest rules of behavior, which are derived from Confucian teaching. It has been argued that the values and prescriptions of these teachings are instilled to Chinese children, even if explicit reference is not made to Confucian context. The important dimensions of this social conditioning process most relevant to our study are those to do with maintaining social and structure harmony... Social harmony is achieved through the key values of Jen *and* Li. Jen *implies human heartedness and acting toward others as one would want to be acted toward.* Li *does not provide explicit rules of behavior (Westwood, 1992) but is about awareness of appropriate behavior in any situation.* Li *serves to structure and maintain relations and order in hierarchies (Ng, 1999).*

Although we have already discussed the Chinese culture we will isolate some of the key relational areas that offer a contrast to the scientific management paradigm of the West but less of a contrast to the emerging Western paradigm of complex adaptive systems management The first and arguably most important area, certainly when thinking about paradigms is moral philosophy. The notion of social harmony, of awareness of Confucian values, of the value of preserving relations, building trust and relating in an obligatory way are all manifestations of this.

> *The Confucian idea is that if every man knows his place and acts in accordance with his position then social order will be ensured. Of the "five cardinal human relationships", four are occupied with the family. They are the relationships between king and subject, between father and son, between husband and wife and those between brothers and between friends. The last relationships can be identified with family because friends are those who can be included within the family circle – "family friends". The family then becomes the starting point for all moral conduct (Lin 1939: 170).*

Even today, when thinking about the Chinese context, there is an overwhelming desire to think of family. Rarely is this notion overlooked and the language of affection and caring connected to family members is often used when explaining organizational relationships. For example, an informal coach at work might very well be an 'auntie or uncle'. In the minds of many workers, especially in Chinese-operated companies, the Chief Executive Officer, CEO, is thought of as the parent or father. In our recent study of

Chinese leadership, the self acclaimed qualities of a leader contained moral imperatives that would be expected of a responsible and revered parent (Wood, et al., 1999).

The concept of family then, is central to the description of a Chinese paradigm. However, whilst the notion of family is etic in nature, (the concept is a more general or universal one [Brislin, 1976]), the socially constructed meaning of the Chinese is emic, (specific to the Chinese culture). Family in the Chinese culture needs to be seen within the web of social and religious norms and values that make up the Chinese social and moral context.

The Chinese psyche can not be explained in a sequential or compartmentalized way. As easily as breathing, Chinese people can simultaneously embrace the tenets of secular Confucianism with its prescriptions for relationships and virtues, the mystical Tao, with its 'go with the flow' nature and a variety of religions such as Buddhism and Catholicism. Above all, the rivers of ancestry flow through the veins of Chinese people. A closer look at some of these tenets reveals that essentially they are paradoxical in their application.

> *We are great enough to make elaborate rules of ceremony but we are also great to treat them as part of the great joke of life...We are great enough to start successive waves of revolution but we are also great enough to compromise and go back to the previous patterns of government... We are great enough to elaborate a perfect system of official impeachment and civil service and traffic regulations and library reading-room rules but we are also great enough to break all systems, ignore them, circumvent them, play with them and become superior to them (Lin 1939:53).*

It is this very quality, the ability to blend even opposites together for practical purposes that is one key to the Chinese nature. Adaptability is more important than allegiance to any one edict. Pragmatism is more important than purity of allegiance. Concepts such as Whitley's (1989) 'utilitarian familism' indicates the ultimate focus that the family takes in the Chinese mind. In this regard, the Chinese environment is less compatible with the scientifically based traditional Western business ethic than with the more fluid and changing complex adaptive systems one (see figure 4).

	Modernism/Scientific Management	Complex Adaptive Systems of Management	Chinese Relational System of Management
P	A rational/economic being	An adaptive, anticipatory and interactive being	An adaptive, family oriented socially responsible being
A	Reward with money-making conditions Calculative psychological Contract*	Reward with adaptation opportunities Collaborative psychological contract	Reward with social approval Family honor and face Cooperative psychological contract
T	Worker as extension of machine/a recipient of orders	Worker as an adaptive organism, co creating solutions	Worker as family member, adapting to contribute to social harmony
O	Develop machines, systems to enhance efficiency: linear thinking	Design relational structures optimize feedback mechanisms	Design family structures and relationships. Minimize Dysfunctional facework
P	Deskilling, specificity of tasks and roles, compliance and obedience	Mix of specificity and discretion Roles flexible and responsive to change	Mix of prescribed rules and social imperatives. Roles contain cultural norms

Figure 4. 'Best fit' Paradigms

Complex adaptive systems, in particular the notion of an enthusiasm for the sort of interaction that is anticipatory, fluid, not always in balance and highly responsive to the other person, are exemplified in all walks of Chinese life, home and work. An example of the sense of loss when this is taken away was evident in the case of a dispersed company, a world name, that operated its computer and information technology from head office (Whiteley, et al., 1991). Head office was in Europe. The policy concerned a wide range of operations, including production plants, engineering works, salesrooms, food factories, in short many different environments.

Previously, discretion allowed people to engage in friendly bargaining, negotiating types of software, hardware and services and above all, relating. Contacts were made, guanxi was built, and relationships strengthened. The new policy, produced in Europe, was rational, standardized across countries, efficient and systematic. It took the form of an automated center. This center became responsible for the range of activities previously performed by people out there in their organizations. In particular, instead of the personal interactions there was a hotline for resolving problems and issues. The whole system was impersonal and distanced. This was not accepted at all by many of the people involved in computer support activities. It got to the stage where, as in our case organization teams were disintegrating and work was being held up.

The complexity, fluidity, spontaneity and even a sense of a family feeling had been taken away, resulting in, from the point of view of the Chinese people, a sterility and impersonality that did not encourage creative solutions, putting in that extra effort and making things work.

The need for a catalyst

If the idea of the complex adaptive systems paradigm is acceptable to the Chinese human resource managers and educators who will be working with their foreign counterparts, then a catalyst is needed to promote it in the human resource setting. The work coming out of Santa Fe, e.g. Holland (1995), and Kauffman (1995) as well as at other centers and in the management field (Stacey, 1996; Stacey, 1998) provides a foundation for thinking about human resource management in a non-scientific relational oriented society. Writers like Stacey have provided a framework for management thinking and practice.

He proposes a sense making model based on the notion of the complex nature of human networks. Central to his theme are notions of understanding. However, it is a particular type of understanding, one that is based on more than simple cause and effect, one that is not constrained by one (scientific) dominant paradigm, one that is not locked into prediction and control and, overall, one that does not seek to bring things back into equilibrium, so that certainty can be recaptured.

Stacey is being joined by an increasing number of management academics who are coming to the conclusion that creativity and the highly sought after competitive edge of the future, has its best environment on the edge of disintegration. Perching on the edge has two benefits. First it releases people from the comfort zone of certainty, in a way that complacency is very difficult to maintain. Secondly it has not descended into disorder where so much uncertainty would exist that no coherent outcomes could be achieved. The ability to contain ambiguities and paradoxes as well as to offload anxieties about not operating in a concrete world ushers in the world of play. When this happens, when ambiguity is accepted, and paradoxes seem to be a natural state of life and when these cease to cause anxiety, then the imaginal world is there to draw on.

How does this relate to Chinese ways? In Chinese ideology, although there have been many dominant and competing ideologies these have not followed the Western pattern of "off with the old and on with the new". A trace of many of these remain in Chinese thinking, often to the consternation of Westerners. It would not be unusual to have filial piety and Confucian conventions integrated into the adoption of, say, Catholicism. This could be done in such a way that festivals such as the hungry ghost and Ching Ming could still be celebrated and, at temples, rituals of sending ancestors off in comfort or keeping in touch, could be engaged in. When pressed for exactitude in defining things from relationships to transactions, an element of ambiguity is often preferred so that when the unforeseen happens, responses can be made to suit developments. The business contract, as it becomes implemented in detail, is a good example of the contrast between predicted certainty and emergent contingencies.

This sense of emergence is so foreign to Western ideology and so natural to Chinese ideology that if there were any difficulties in rising to new paradigms such as complex adaptive systems and the complex learning they encourage, then they would be more keenly felt in the West.

7. References

Abrahamson, E. Management fashion. *Academy of Management Review* 21, 1, 254-285, 1996.

Adler, N. *International Dimensions of Organizational Behaviour* Boston, Massachusetts: PWS-Kent, 1991.

Ansoff, I. and McDonnell, E. *Implanting Strategic Management.* New York: Prentice-Hall Int. Ltd, 1990.

Ansoff, I. Critique of Henry Mintzberg's 'The Design School': Reconsidering the basic premises of strategic Management. *Strategic Management Journal,* 12, 449-461, 1991.

Antoniou, P., and Whitman, K. Understanding Chinese interpersonal norms and effective management of Sino-Western joint ventures. *Multinational Business Review,* 6, 1, 53-62, 1998.

Barley, S., and Kunda G. Design and Devotion: Surges of Rational and Normative Ideologies of Control in Managerial Discourse. *Administrative Science Quarterly,* 37, 363-399, 1992.

Bartlett, C., and Ghoshal, S. *Building Structure in Managers' Minds.* In H. Mintzberg and J. Quinn. *The Strategy Process: Concepts, contexts and cases.* Upper Saddle River, N.J.: Prentice Hall, 1996.

Bond, M. *The Psychology of the Chinese People.* Hong Kong: Oxford Uni. Press, 1986.

Briggs, J., and Peat, F. *Turbulent Mirror: An Illustrated Guide to Chaos Theory and the Science of Wholeness.* New York: Harper & Row, 1989.

Brislin, R. Comparative Research Methodology: Cross-cultural Studies. *International Journal of Psychology* 2, 389-444, 1976.

Brown, S., and Eisenhardt, K. *Competing on the Edge: Strategy as Structured Chaos*. Boston: Harvard Business School Press, 1998.

Bjorkman, I., and Lu Y. A corporate perspective on the management of human resources in China. *Journal of World Business,* 34, 1, 16-25, 1999

Cacioppe, R., and Mock, P. Developing the police officer at work. *Leadership and Organization Development Journal.* 6, 5, 3-48, 1985.

Carless, S., Mann, L., and Wearing, A. Leadership, managerial performance and 360-degree feedback. *Applied Psychology – An International Review* 47, 4, 481-496, 1998.

Carlopio, J., Andrewartha, G., and Armstrong, H. *Developing management skills in Australia.* Melbourne, Longman, 1997.

Champy, J. *Reengineering management: The mandate for new leadership.* London, Harper Collins, 1995.

Chang, H. and Holt. G. An exploration of interpersonal relationships in two Taiwanese computer firms. *Human Relations* 49, 12, 1489 –1518, 1996.

Cheng, L. and Lu, C. *Transnational consortiums: Their development, trends and characteristics.* Beijing: International Technology and Economy Institute, 1992 (English version 1993).

Cheng, L., & Zhang, S. *Discussion on Influencing Science-Technology Development by Establishing the Market System of Socialist Economy.* Selected Excerpts from Research Papers: International Technology and Economy Institute, 1995 (English version 1996).

Chia, R. Essay: Thirty Years On: From organisational structures to the organisation of thought. *Organisation Studies* 18, 4, 685-707, 1997.

Child, J. *The Management of Joint Ventures in China.* Beijing, European Community Management Institute, 1990.

Chin, M. *Asian management systems: Chinese, Japanese and Korean styles of business.* London: International Thomson Business Press, 1995.

Chow, G. *Understanding China's economy.* Singapore: World Scientific, 1994.

Chu, C. On the Shame orientation of the Chinese. *Symposium on the Character of the Chinese: An interdisciplinary approach.* Taipei: Institute of Ethnology, Academia Sinica, 1973.

Covey, S. *Principle-Centred Leadership.* London, Simon and Schuster, 1992

Cui, G. The evolutionary process of global market expansion: experiences of MNCs in China. *Journal of World Business,* 33, 1, 87-110, 1998.

Daft, R., Lengel, R., and Trevino, L. Message equivocality, media selection, and manager performance; Implications for information systems. MIS Quarterly 11, 3, 354-366, 1987.

Deal, T. and Kennedy, A. *Corporate Cultures: The Rites and Rituals of Corporate Life.* London, Penguin, 1982.

Dowling, P. *International Dimensions of Human Resource Management* (2nd edition) Belmont, California: Wadsworth, 1994.

Drucker, P. *The Practice of Management.* New York, Harper and Row, 1954.

Emery, F. *Participative Design for Participative Democracy.* Canberra, Centre for Continuing Education, ANU, 1993.

Etzioni, A. *A Comparative Analysis of Complex Organizations.* New York, Free Press, 1971.

Ferraro, G. *The cultural dimension of international business.* New Jersey: Prentice Hall, 1998.

Frost, P., Moore, L., Reis, L., Lundberg, C., and Martin, J. *Reframing Organisational Culture,* Newbury Park: Sage, 1991.

Fung, Y. *A Short History of Chinese Philosophy.* New York, The Free Press, 1948/1997.

Gerth, H., and Mills, C. *From Max Weber: Essays in sociology.* New York: Oxford University Press, 1946.

Gilbreth, F. *Motion Study.* New York, Van Nostrand, 1911.

Gleick, J. *Chaos: The amazing science of the unpredictable.* London, Minerva, 1996.

Guest, D. Human resource management and industrial relations. *Journal of Management Studies* 24, 5, 149-176, 1987.

Han, P. *Human Relations at Work in the Confucian Culture.* Second International Organisational Behavior Teaching Conference, Perth, Western Australia, Curtin University, 1992.

Hayles, N. *Chaos and Order: Complex Dynamics in Literature and Science.* Chicago/London, University of Chicago Press, 1994.

Herzberg, F. *Work and the Nature of Man.* Cleveland, Ohio: World Publishing, 1966.

Hofstede, G. *Culture's Consequences: International differences in work related values.* Beverley Hills, Sage, 1980.

Holland, J. *Hidden order: How adaptation builds complexity.* Reading, M.A: Helix Books, Addison Wesley Publishing Co, 1995.

International Survey Research Corporation. Research provides performance benchmark for foreign firms in China *Asian Business* 32, 11, 64, 1996.

Jantsch, E. *The Self Organising Universe.* Oxford, Pergamon, 1980.

Jaques, E. *Requisite Organisation: The CEO's Guide to Creative Structure and Leadership* USA: Cason Hall and Co, 1989.

Kanter, R. *The Change Masters: Innovations for Productivity in the American Corporation.* London, Allen and Unwin, 1984.

Kauffman, S. Antichaos and adaptation. *Scientific American* 265, 2, 64-70, 1991.

Khong, E., and Trigo, V. *Breaking the "Iron Rice Bowl": An empirical study on workers' views and labor relations in China-Guangzhou.* In Proceedings of the Second South China International Business Symposium, Macau, University of Macau, 1996.

Kitay, J., and Lansbury R. *Human Resource Management and Industrial Relations in an era of Global Markets: Australian and international Trends* In Proceedings of an EPAC roundtable held in Canberra on 6 February 1995. Canberra, EPAC, Australian Government Publishing Service, 1995.

Kitay, J. *Changing patterns of employment relations: Theoretical and methodological framework for six Australian industry studies.* In J. Kitay and R.

Lansbury. *Changing Employment Relations in Australia.* Melbourne, Oxford University Press: 1-43, 1997.

Ko, E. Lessons in leadership. *Asian Business.* 34, 2, 53-55, 1998.

Lasserre, P., and Schuette, H. *Strategies for Asia Pacific.* London, Macmillan Press, 1995.

Legge, K. A New Realism? The Politico-economic context of personnel management 1979-87. *Personnel Management in Recession and Recovery: A comparative analysis of what the surveys say.* Bradford, MCB University Press, 1988.

Lewin, K. *Field Theory in Social Science: Selected Theoretical Papers.* New York: Harper and Row, 1951.

Lin, Y. *My country and my people.* Surrey: Heinemann, 1939.

Ling, W., Chen, L., & Wang, D. The construction of the CPM scale for leadership behavior assessment. *Acta Psychologica Sinica,* 19, 199-207, 1987.

Lupton, T. Best Fit in the Design of Organisations. *Personnel Review,* 4, 1, 15-30, 1975.

Markel, D. Finally, a national labor law. *China Business Review,* 21, 6, 46-49, 1994.

Maslow, A. *Motivation and personality.* New York, Harper & Row, 1970.

Maxfield, R. Complexity and Organization Management. In D. Alberts, and T. Czerwinski (eds) *Complexity, global politics and national security* Washington: National Defense University, 1999.

Mayo, E. *A New Approach ot Industrial Relations.* Boston: Division of Research, Graduate School of Business Administration, Harvard University, 1930.

McGreal, I. *Great thinkers of the eastern world: The major thinkers and the philosophical and religious classics of China, India, Japan, Korea and the world of Islam.* New York: Harper Collins, 1995.

McGregor, D. *The Human Side of Enterprise.* New York, McGraw Hill, 1960.

Miles, R., and Snow, C. *Organizational Strategy, Structure and Process.* New York, McGraw Hill, 1978.

Mintzberg, H. *Strategy Making in Three Modes*. In J. Quinn, H. Mintberg, and R. James. *The Strategy Process: Concepts, Contexts and Cases*. Englewood CLiffs, N.J., Prentice Hall International, 1988.

Morgan, G. Paradigms, Metaphors and Puzzle Solving in Organisational Theory. *Adminstrative Science Quarterly*, 25, 605-622, 1980.

Morgan, G. *Images of Organization: the executive edition*. San Francisco, Berrett-Koehler, 1997.

Nadler, D., and Nadler, M. *Champions of Change: How CEOs and their companies are mastering the skills of radical change*. San Francisco, Josey-Bass Publishers, 1998.

Nankervis, A., Compton, R., and McCarthy, T. *Strategic Human Resource Management*. Melbourne, International Thomson Publishing Company, 1999.

Negandhi, A., and Prasad, R. *Comparative Management*. New York, Appleton-Century-Crofts, 1971.

Ng, P. *Philosophy and Business Management Critical Paper*. Faculty of Business. Hong Kong, Curtin and Lingnan: Paper in Partial Completion of DBA, 1999.

Nicholson International. Answering China's human resource challenges *Asiamoney*, 8, 10, 31-35, 1998.

Pascale, R. *Managing on the Edge: How successful firms use conflict to stay ahead*. London, Viking Penguin, 1990.

Pettigrew, A. *Issues of time and site selection in longitudinal research on change*. In Cash, J. and Lawrence, P. Eds *The Information Systems Research Challenge: Qualitative Research Methods*. Boston, Massachusetts: Harvard Press: 13-19, 1989.

Pondy, L., Frost, P., Morgan, G., and Dandridge, T. *Organisational Symbolism*. Greenwich C.T., JAI Press, 1983.

Porter, M. *Competitive strategy: Techniques for analyzing industries and competitors*. New York: The Free Press, 1980.

Porter, M. *Competitive Advantage: Creating and Sustaining Superior Performance*. New York, The Free Press, 1985.

Prigogine, I. *The End of Uncertainty: Tme, Chaos and the New Laws of Nature.* New York, The Free Press, 1996.

Roeland, J. (ed) *Autopoiesis and Configuration Theory: New Approaches to Societal Steering.* Dordrecht, Kluwer Academic Publishers, 1991.

Roethlisberger, F., and Dixon W. *Management and the Worker.* Cambridge, Harvard University Press, 1939.

Rosen, D. *Behind the open door: Foreign enterprises in the Chinese marketplace.* Washington: Institute for International Economics, 1999.

Scarborough, J. Comparing Chinese and western cultural roots: Why east is east and... *Business Horizons*, November, 15-24, 1998.

Schein, E. *Organisational Culture and Leadership.* San Francisco: Jossey Bass, 1985.

Schein, E. On dialogue, culture and organizational learning. *Organisational Dynamics* 22, 2, 40-52, 1993.

Schuler, R. Personnel and Human Resource Management Choices and Organizational Strategy. *Human Resource Planning* 10, 1, 1-17, 1989.

Schuler, R., and Jackson, S. Linking Competitive Strategies with Human Resource Management. *Academy of Management Executive* 1, 3, 207-219, 1987.

Scott, W. The Adolescence of Institutional Theory. *Administrative Science Quarterly* 32, 4, 493-511, 1987.

Scruton, R. *Modern Philosophy: an introduction and survey.* London, Arrow Books, 1997.

Senge, P. Mental Models. *Planning Review* 20, 2, 5, 1992.

Stacey, R. *Complexity and Creativity in Organisations.* San Francisco, Berrett Koehler, 1996.

Stacey, R. Emerging strategies for a chaotic environment. *Long Range Planning* 29, 2, 182-189, 1998.

Swaak, R. The role of human resources in China. *Compensation and Benefits Review*, 27, 5, 39-46, 1995.

Sweeney, E. *Human Resource Management Implications.* The Second International Business Symposium: Managing Business in the Twenty First Century, Macau, University of Macau, 1996.

Tang, S., Cheng, L., Lai, E., and Zhang, S. *Human Resource Strategies and Practices in Foreign Invested Enterprises in the People's Republic of China.* Hong Kong, Hong Kong Institute of Human Resources and International Technology and Economy Institute, 1996.

Tang, S., Lai, E., Nankervis, A., and Morrissey, B. *Human Resource Management Strategies And Practices In Australia.* Hong Kong, Institute of Human Resources, 1996.

Tang, S. *The Mass Transit Railway Corporation: cultivating a customer service culture to create competitive advantage.* In A. Whiteley. *Managing Change: A Core Values Approach.* Melbourne, Macmillan, 1996.

Tang, S., and Whiteley, A. *Management cases in Hong Kong.* Hong Kong: Longman, 1990.

Tarnas, R. *The Passion of the Western Mind: Understanding the ideas that have shaped our world view.* New York, Ballantine Books, 1991.

Taylor, F. *The Principles of Scientific Management.* New York, Harper Row, 1929.

Torrington, D., Mackay, H., and Hall, J. "The Changing Nature of Personnel Management." *Employee Relations* 7, 5, 10-16, 1985.

Torrington, D., and Huat, T. *Human Resource Management for South East Asia.* New York: Prentice Hall, 1994.

Trompenaars, F., and Hampden-Turner, C. *Riding the waves of culture: Understanding cultural diversity in business.* London: Nicholas Brealey, 1998.

Tsoukas, H. Introduction: Chaos, Complexity & Organisational Theory. *Organization*, 5, 3, 291-314, 1998.

Tyson, S. *Human Resource Strategy: Towards a general theory of Human Resource Management.* London, Pitman, 1995.

Waldrop, M. *Complexity: The Emerging Science at the Edge of Order and Chaos.* London, Viking, 1992.

Walker, J. *Human Resource Strategy.* Sydney, McGraw-Hill, 1992.

Weisbord, M. *Productive Workplaces: Organising and Managing for Dignity, Meaning and Community*. San Francisco, Jossey Bass, 1987.

Wheatley, M. *Leadership and the New Science: Learning about Organisation from an Orderly Universe*. San Francisco, C.A., Sage, 1994.

Whetton, D. and Cameron, K. *Developing Management Skills*. New York, HarperCollins, 1991.

Whiteley, A. Managing Change the UK Way: Vocational and Management Education and Training in Britain. *Journal of Human Resource Management*: 41-51, 1988.

Whiteley, A. and Jordan, E. Behavioural aspects of introducing change in information systems. *Australia Computer Journal* 22, 2, 58-68, 1991.

Whiteley, A. *Managing Change: A Core Values Approach*. Melbourne, Macmillan, 1995.

Whiteley, A., Cheung, S., Zhang, S., and So, W. *Human resource management in foreign invested companies in the People's Republic of China*. Hong Kong, Hong Kong Institute of Human Resource Management, 1997.

Whiteley, A. *Sustainable Change: A Case on the Waterfront*. Perth, Australia, Vine Publishing, 1999a.

Whiteley, A. Systemic Barriers to Managing Change: Is Autopoiesis an Appropriate Metaphor? *Journal of the Australian and New Zealand Academy of Management*, 1999b.

Whiteley, A. *PATOP as a readiness for strategic decision making and change: An Occasional Paper for Advanced Theory in Business Seminar Series*. Curtin Graduate School of Business, 1999c.

Whitley, R. On the nature of managerial tasks and skills: their distinguishing characteristics and organisation. *Journal of Management Studies* 26, 3, 209-225, 1989.

Wong, C., and Law, K. Managing localization of human resources in the PRC: a practical model. *Journal of World Business* 34, 1, 26-37, 1999.

Wood, E., Whiteley, A., and Zhang, S. *Guanxi in Chinese leadership: Initial perceptions of State-owned and Foreign-invested enterprise leaders.* Academy of International Business South East Asia Region Conference, Melbourne, 1999.

Wu, C. *On grand strategy in a broad sense: Selected excerpts from research papers.* Beijing, International Technology and Economy Institute, 1992.

Yau, O. Chinese Cultural Values: Their Dimensions and Marketing Implications. *European Journal of Marketing* 22, 5, 44-57, 1988.

Zhao, S. Human resource management implications of managing business change in China. *Proceedings of the Second South China International Business Symposium, Macau* 963-973, 1996

Zohar, D. and Marshall, I. *The Quantum Society: Mind Physics and a new social vision.* London, Hammersmith, 1994.

Index

"1 + 1 = 3"	16
Alignment of HR strategies and practices with business strategies	31
Aristotle	26
Asian financial crisis	45
Business strategy	55-73
Business strategy findings	76
Business strategy theory and concepts	68
Chaos	23, 25, 176
China Competency Model	17
Chinese relational characteristics	37, 169, 179
Co-evolution	176
Co-creation model	17
Collective intelligence	22
Communication of strategy	84
Compatible paradigms	169
Competing value systems	63, 93
Complex Adaptive Systems	23, 61, 169, 174, 175, 179, 182
Complexity theory	23, 177
Confucianism	21, 31
Confucius	25, 33, 34
Corporate culture	92, 94, 95
Current economic situation in China	39
Descartes	27, 29
Employment protection legislation	10
Etic/emic categorization	70
Evolutionary trajectories	176
"face"	59, 74, 109
Family system	176
Guanxi	59, 74, 133, 134, 182
History of personnel management in China	7
HR function in foreign invested enterprises	115
His Chu	34
Human resource management activities	99
Human resource management practices	118
Human resource strategies in the Chinese context	89
Human resource strategies in the context of business strategy	55

Innovation   16, 73, 81
Internal-focus approach   15

"job-hopping"   12, 138, 139

Labor relations   56
Lao Tzu   35
Linear systems approach to management   1, 17, 74, 100, 170, 172, 173

Mao Zedong   36
Mencius   34
Mianxi and lien   92
Mo   35
Modern conception of HRM   170
Moral character   21, 26, 57, 60, 120
Mozi   35

Newton   27

Open door policy   2, 3, 10, 11, 42
Organizational culture   93, 94, 105, 132, 156

PATOP model   172, 178
Plato   26
Postmodernists   28
Protestant work ethic   23, 58, 64
Punctuated equilibrium   177

Quality of the labour force   46

Scientific management   36, 64, 65, 99, 172, 174, 178, 181
Shared values   30
Socio-technical systems   102
Socrates   26, 29
Strategic human resource management   1, 67, 97, 98, 104, 114
Sun Yat-sen   36

Tan Sitong   36
"three irons"   8, 9, 122
Transitional period   36, 62, 101, 103
Typologies of business strategy   13, 15, 77

utilitarian familism   180

Values   95

Western ideology   25
Western orthodoxy   23, 55, 57, 119, 169
Western versus Chinese (Confucian)   20

ideologies
Wittgenstein   29
World Trade Organization   2, 3, 52, 53

Xunzi   35